SRA

Reading Mastery

Signature Edition

Teacher's Guide
Grade K

Siegfried Engelmann
Elaine C. Bruner

McGraw Hill SRA

Columbus, OH

SRAonline.com

 SRA

Send all inquiries to this address:
SRA/McGraw-Hill
4400 Easton Commons
Columbus, OH 43219

Printed in the United States of America.

ISBN: 978-0-07-612220-2
MHID: 0-07-612220-4

21 LMN 19

■■■■■■■■■■ Contents ■■■■■■■■■■

NOTE TO THE TEACHER

Your hard work in practicing these *Reading Mastery* tasks will provide you with a valuable set of skills for working with children of all abilities. You will learn how to present and how to correct so that children can master critical skills. You may be surprised to find the correction techniques you learn are often important in working with higher-performing children. If you have mastered the techniques, no child in your beginning reading classroom will fail to learn to read. By achieving this goal, you will provide a valuable service both to your community and to the children.

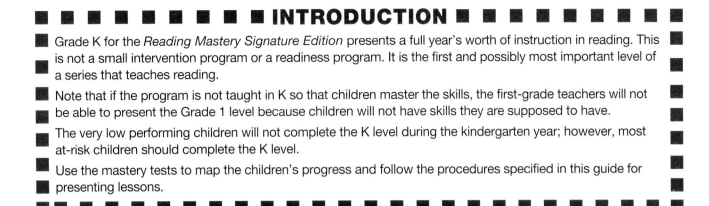

■ Grade K for the *Reading Mastery Signature Edition* presents a full year's worth of instruction in reading. This is not a small intervention program or a readiness program. It is the first and possibly most important level of a series that teaches reading.

■ Note that if the program is not taught in K so that children master the skills, the first-grade teachers will not be able to present the Grade 1 level because children will not have skills they are supposed to have.

■ The very low performing children will not complete the K level during the kindergarten year; however, most at-risk children should complete the K level.

■ Use the mastery tests to map the children's progress and follow the procedures specified in this guide for presenting lessons.

Reading Mastery Signature Edition, Grade K is a beginning reading program that teaches all the skills non-reading children need to master the basics of beginning reading. When children complete Grade K, they go into *Reading Mastery* Grade 1, which is designed to mesh perfectly with the skills the children have acquired in *Reading Mastery* Grade K. The concept underlying *Reading Mastery* is that virtually all children can learn if we teach them carefully. The program therefore attempts to provide the kind of careful instruction that is needed to teach basic skills. Another assumption of the program is that this instruction will be implemented only if the teacher does what is required to ensure that the children master each skill.

Like many other programs, *Reading Mastery* K includes prereading exercises, activities associated with beginning decoding, work with symbol identification, rhyming, comprehension activities, and so forth. Unlike many other programs, however, *Reading Mastery* K presents each of these activities in a carefully programmed sequence.

1. The exercises are structured as simply as possible. The vocabulary used by the teacher is reduced. The procedures that are followed with one exercise are followed with a similar exercise so that the children can see how the exercises are the same.

2. The practice the children receive is carefully controlled and realistic. For example, symbols like **b**, **m**, and **t** are introduced at the rate of one every three or four lessons so that the children receive enough practice to master each of the symbols. The practice for every other skill the children are taught is controlled in a similar way.

3. The sequence of skills is structured so that the children master all the skills they need for later, more complicated tasks. The prereading activities in *Reading Mastery* K are unique. The purpose of prereading activities is to ensure that every skill needed for beginning decoding is taught, and only those skills are taught. No activity is introduced because it "might" help the children. The prereading exercises focus on the specific behaviors the children will use when they begin decoding words.

4. A final aspect of the program design has to do with the teacher's behavior. What the teacher does and says is specified. The teacher is not given general instructions; rather, the teacher is provided with the exact words that are to be used when presenting each of the tasks. Other behaviors—pointing, signaling the group to respond, and the like—are specified precisely. The program indicates where the children are likely to make mistakes and precisely what the teacher should do to correct each mistake.

The reason for the attention to detail in the design of the program is that details make a difference. Well-intentioned teachers frequently confuse children, particularly lower-performing children, with explanations that are beyond the children's understanding. General teaching suggestions don't give the teacher enough direction and frequently lead to activities that don't reach every child. Poorly sequenced exercises may further confuse the children, delay their learning, and perhaps result in their losing interest in reading.

The *Reading Mastery* K program prevents these problems from developing. A teacher who follows the program carefully will be able to teach children who would be likely to fail if less care were used.

Does it follow that the program is appropriate only for low performers? Not at all. It is appropriate for any child—regardless of age—who has not mastered the basic decoding and comprehension skills. It is designed for the bright and curious child, as well as for the slower-learning child. For students with limited English language proficiency, it is recommended that they receive instruction in language skills before starting *Reading Mastery* Grade K.

Children can proceed through the program as fast as they are capable of moving. It is designed so that children who perform well can skip specified lessons. Full-day kindergartners can complete the program by April if they begin in September. The extremely low performers will probably not complete the entire program by the end of the school year, although they should have mastered at least 130 of the 160 lessons. The very highest performing children should be placed, if possible, in *Reading Mastery*: Fast Cycle, an accelerated reading program.

PROGRAM MATERIALS

The following materials are intended for your use. They are included in the kit:

1. *Three Presentation Books.* These books specify each activity in each lesson and tell you how to present it. Planning Pages appear every 20 lessons. These present an overview of the skills taught, a summary of special considerations for upcoming lessons, and additional reading activities.

2. *The Teacher's Guide.* Included in this guide are an explanation of the program, the placement test for the initial placement of the children, and instructions on how to teach the program.

3. *The Spelling Presentation Book.* This book contains spelling lessons, which begin at lesson 50 and continue through the remainder of the program.

4. A copy of the Storybook that the children use.

5. A *Workbook Answer Key.*

6. A *Skills Profile Folder,* which summarizes the skills taught in the program and provides a space for indicating when a child has mastered each skill. One folder is needed for each child.

7. A *compact disk* demonstrating how to pronounce the sounds and how to present exercises from the program.

8. A *plastic transparency page protector* to enable you to write on the pages of the Presentation Book when necessary.

9. A set of *group progress indicators* to enable you to keep track of the place each group has reached in the program.

Each child should have the following:

1. A *Storybook* (hardbound and reusable). This book contains the stories for lessons 91 to 160.

2. A set of three Workbooks (consumable). These workbooks contain written activities for every lesson.

3. Optional: *Independent Readers. Reading Mastery,* Grade K has optional Independent Readers. See page 59.

TIME REQUIREMENTS FOR READING

Lessons should be scheduled on every available school day. The children are divided into small, homogeneous groups for instruction (see page 11). The teacher and student times required each day for all of the reading activities are as follows:

Activity	Teacher Time	Student Time
Group Instruction	25–30 minutes for each group	25–30 minutes for each group
Independent Work	————	15–20 minutes for each group
Work Check	5 minutes for each group	————
Spelling (Lessons 50–160)	10 minutes for all groups if lesson is presented to entire class	

Note: The spelling activities are highly recommended if your daily schedule includes spelling.

COORDINATION OF READING AND LANGUAGE

Engaging students in a language program will increase success in the reading program. There are two important rules for effectively coordinating reading and language.

1. Children are never to read something they would be unable to understand if it were presented verbally. Children should not read words, sentences, or stories they wouldn't understand if somebody said those items.

2. Language instruction must stay ahead of reading instruction on the beginning levels. You should never have to stop and explain the meaning of a word while students are engaged in beginning reading. Later, when children have advanced to reading second-grade-level material they will read to learn new ideas and the meaning of unfamiliar words. During instruction in Grade K and Grade 1, however, the children's language skills must stay ahead of what they are decoding so they always understand what they read.

Procedures For Scheduling Language And Reading In Grade K

Reading Mastery Signature Edition, Grade K Language may be introduced as a support program for beginning reading.

1. If children place at lesson 1, 11, 21, or 31 of *Reading Mastery* Language, do not begin teaching reading until students have completed lesson 40 and have passed the lesson 40 test.

2. Use the period designated for reading as a second language period until children complete lesson 40; then continue with one language period and one reading period each day.

Do not have language and reading periods back to back.

The amount of language material that you cover each day will depend on how much practice children need to achieve mastery. If children do not completely master an entire lesson during the first language period, review it during the second language period and start on the next language lesson if time permits. Expect children who place at lesson 1 to go the slowest, and children who place at 31 to go the fastest.

Most children should be able to average about two language lessons a day, which means that even the slower children who start at lesson 1 will require about 30 school days to complete preparation for reading.

Children who place at language lesson 11 will require only about 15 days to complete the program through lesson 40. Children who place at lesson 21 should finish it in less than 10 days. Those who place at 31 should require only 2 or 3 days to complete it.

After children pass the language test for lesson 40, convert one of the daily language periods into a daily reading period. Continue to provide a daily period in reading and in language.

For children who have limited or no English, follow the recommendations in the *Reading Mastery,* Grade K Language Teacher's Guide.

Decoding

Reading Mastery introduces children to a sounding–out analysis of words, starting with Lesson 28. Teaching the children to sound out words has these advantages:

1. Children learn more words from a given amount of teaching. If children are taught ten words as sight words, the children are capable of reading only ten words. If children learn ten symbols introduced in *Reading Mastery* as sounds, they are capable of reading over a thousand regularly spelled words composed of those sounds.

2. The emphasis on sounds assures that children attend to the details of the words, or how the words are spelled. This information becomes very important when children are confronted with words that are similar in "shape," such as: **when, then, where,** and **there.**

3. Although the sounding-out procedure is replaced with a procedure for reading the fast way, beginning with lesson 75 the sounding-out procedure serves as an important back-up, particularly when children read independently. By using the sounding-out procedure, the children can verify the pronunciation of words that they may not be able to identify by sight.

Before children begin sounding out words, they work on the *preskills.* These are the oral skills and the symbol-identification skills that are needed when children sound out a word by identifying each symbol in a word as a "sound" and saying the word fast. By lesson 28 children have learned six sounds in isolation. They practice saying words slowly and saying them fast. They also practice rhyming by starting with different beginning sounds and saying a specified word ending. Finally, they practice sequencing events so that they develop a general skill of combining the "first event" with the "next event."

Throughout the program children continue to practice skills that have been taught earlier. For instance, after lesson 28, children continue to practice rhyming, symbol identification of earlier-taught sounds, and oral blending. Also, after lesson 75, children continue to read some words by sounding them out.

Note that as part of the word-reading practice, children learn words that are "irregular" as well as regularly spelled words. The word **was** is irregular because it is pronounced in a way that is not predicted by the sounds of the individual letters. (The word **was** does not rhyme with **bass,** which is what it would do if it were regular.)

Comprehension

Just as the decoding skills are sequenced so that the children work first on easy examples and then on more difficult applications, the comprehension skills are also sequenced. Comprehension skills such as picture comprehension and sequencing events are presented before children engage in word reading.

After children are introduced to story reading, they answer questions while reading the story. When the story is completed, the students predict what the story picture will show. They then answer questions about the story picture. Children are introduced to written comprehension items starting with lesson 120. These items become increasingly complex as the children become more skilled.

Finally, games that require the students to follow instructions are introduced at lesson 151. To play these games, the children must read carefully and must understand what they read.

For activities that relate to decoding and comprehension, see the following charts.

PROGRAM ACTIVITIES THAT RELATE TO WORD DECODING

Prereading Lessons 1–27	Sounding out words Lessons 28–74	Reading words the fast way Lessons 75–160
Sound pronunciation		
Sequencing		

Oral blending
    Saying words slowly
    Saying words fast		

Rhyming		
Symbol identification (as sounds)	Symbol identification	Symbol identification
	Reading vocabulary (word lists)	Reading vocabulary
	Story reading	Story reading
		Individual Fluency Checkouts for rate and accuracy
Independent workbook practice	Independent workbook practice	Independent workbook practice

PROGRAM ACTIVITIES THAT RELATE TO COMPREHENSION

Prereading Lessons 1–27	Beginning reading Lessons 28–160
Picture comprehension	Comprehension of vocabulary words
Sequencing events	Oral comprehension questions about sentences in stories
	Story pictures
	Written comprehension activities
	Comprehension games

Written Work

The children begin their work on worksheets (perforated sheets bound in workbook form) on the first day of the program. The worksheets provide up to 20 minutes a day of independent work that relates to the skills the children are learning in the program. Lead the children through each new kind of exercise for a few days; then have the children do the exercises independently. Worksheet activities include picture completion, sound-writing practice on the new sounds, work with pattern recognition, and matching exercises. Reading comprehension and picture comprehension exercises relate to the stories the children are reading. Many of the activities prepare the children for taking standardized tests.

The written work also provides a means of teaching the children to work independently. After new skills are introduced, the children complete their worksheets by themselves. This allows you time to work with the other groups.

Spelling

The spelling lessons start when the children reach lesson 50 in the program. The spelling activities begin with the children writing individual sounds from your dictation. Later the children write words and sentences that you dictate. Spelling words follow the sequence of reading words taught in the program.

Spelling is a very important skill for the children to master. It can be taught to the entire class (if your schedule does not give you time to teach it to small groups) when the lowest-performing group reaches lesson 40. The *Spelling Presentation Book* is a separate component of *Reading Mastery* and is included in the teacher's materials.

ORGANIZATION OF THE PROGRAM

Reading Mastery, Grade K has two main sections: Prereading Skills and Reading. Each section is organized into tracks (such as Say It Fast or Sounds), formats, and tasks. Each *track* extends through several lessons. A *format* is one segment of a track—one step in the programming of a skill. It is a pattern of teaching steps repeated in a number of successive lessons.

Here, for example, is a format that provides a pattern for a series of exercises:

Children say it fast
a. Let's play Say It Fast.
b. (Hold out your hand.) Listen. (First part of word) (Pause.) (Second part of word) Say it fast! (Drop your hand.) *The children respond.*

By putting different words into the format, or pattern, several exercises are created:

Ice (pause) **cream.** Say it fast!
Sis (pause) **ter.** Say it fast!
Ham (pause) **burger.** Say it fast!

Such a series of exercises has these advantages:

1. The children master a skill by practicing it with many different examples.

2. The children can see the similarity between various exercises in the same track.

3. You learn the presentation once, then use it many times, thus conserving your time and effort.

USING THE PRESENTATION BOOK

Each of the three Presentation Books provides you with directions for presenting each exercise and also provides display material for the children. For example, some of the exercises involve identifying symbols. The symbols the children respond to are included in the Presentation Books.

The Presentation Books are divided into lessons. The number of the lesson appears at the top and bottom of every page. The first page of the lesson is indicated by the word *Lesson* preceding the number; the last page is indicated by the words *End of Lesson* at the bottom of the page.

In each lesson the track headings (such as Sounds, Say It Fast, or Symbol Action) are printed in boldface capitals. If a track has not been presented before, its title is preceded by a red star ★. The track titles will tell you at a glance the skill to be developed in the exercises that follow. The exercises are numbered and the number is followed by a brief description of that exercise's objective.

What you are to say is in blue type. What you are to do is in black type in parentheses. The oral responses expected from the children are in italics. Expected motor responses are also in italics. Frequently the children's response is followed by your repetition of the response as a reinforcement for the children. Each small letter (**a, b, c,** and so on) indicates a new step in the development of the exercise. Everything that you will need to say and do in teaching the exercise is specified in these steps, together with the children's correct responses.

While the children are working from examples in the Presentation Book, be sure to hold it so that every child in the group can see it. When pointing to or touching examples in the book, do not cover with your hand or arm anything that the children need to see. When you reach the portion of each lesson that need not be displayed (such as the stories and worksheet directions) you will still need to have the book before you so that you can follow the directions for teaching these activities.

As you progress through the lessons, you will notice that some of the exercise titles have lines above and below them. The lines signal the introduction of a new format. Since the tracks are all very tightly sequenced, there may be minor changes in a format that are not signaled by using lines; be alert for such changes and implement them in your presentation. When you see the lines, however, you will be alerted to a major change in the method of presenting the exercise. Be careful not to continue the pattern of the old format.

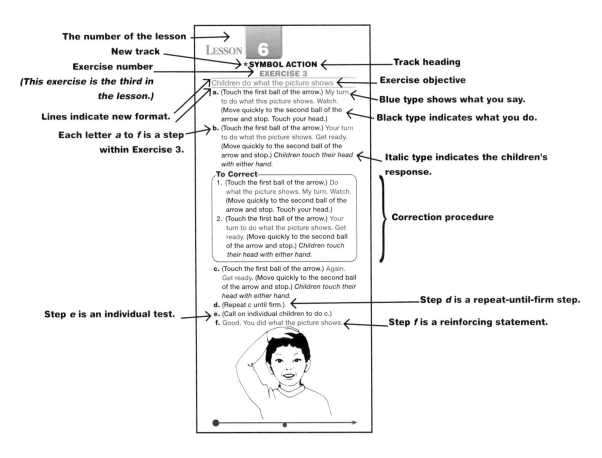

PART 1

Task 1   Total possible: 2 points

(Circle 1 point on the scoring sheet for each correct response at *b* and *c*.)

This is an oral task. For step *c,* say the sound **d,** not the letter name.

a. You're going to say some sounds.
b. **(test item)** Say (pause) **rrr.** *rrr.*
c. **(test item)** Now say (pause) **d.** *d.*

Task 2   Total possible: 10 points

(Circle 1 point on the scoring sheet for each correct response at *b.*)

a. (Point to the sounds.) These are sounds. (Point to the boxed **m.**) This sound is (pause) **mmm.** What sound? (Touch **m.**) *mmm.*
b. **(test items)** (Point to each unboxed sound in the column. For each sound, ask:) Is this (pause) **mmm?**

(Circle 1 point on the scoring sheet for each correct response at step *d.*)

c. (Point to the boxed **a.**) This sound is (pause) **ăăă.** What sound? (Touch **a.**) *ăăă.*
d. **(test items)**)Point to each unboxed sound in the column. For each sound, ask:) Is this (pause) **ăăă?**

Task 3   Total possible: 4 points

(Circle 2 points on the scoring sheet for each correct response at *b* and *c*.)

a. Let's play Say It Fast. Listen. **Ice** (pause) **box.** I can say it fast. **Icebox.**
b. **(test item)** Listen. **Foot** (pause) **ball.** (Pause.) Say it fast. *Football.* Yes, **football.**
c. **(test item)** Here's another word. Listen. (Pause.) **Nnnōōōzzz.** (Pause.) Say it fast. *Nose.* Yes, **nose.**

Task 4   Total possible: 4 points

(Circle 2 points on the scoring sheet for each correct response at *b* and *d*.)

(This is an oral task. Do not stop between the sounds when saying *zzzoooo* or *wwwēēē*.)

a. First I'll say a word slowly. Then you'll say that word slowly. I'll say (Pause) **zoo** slowly. Listen. (Pause.) **Zzzoooo.**
b. **(test item)** Your turn. Say (pause) **zzzoooo.** *Zzzoooo.*
    (A child scores 2 points if he or she says the correct sounds without stopping between the sounds.)
c. Now I'll say (pause) **wē** slowly. Listen. (pause.) **Wwwēēē.**
d. **(test item)** Your turn. Say (pause) **wwwēēē.** (A child scores 2 points if he or she says the correct sounds without stopping between the sounds.)

Add the number of points the child earned on part 1. Note: Administer part 2 **only** to children who made 19 or 20 points on part 1.

PART 2

Task 1   Total possible: 4 points

(Circle 2 points on the scoring sheet for each correct response at *a* and *b*.)

a. **(test item)** Point to the boxed **m.**) Let's see if you remember this sound. (Pause.) What sound? (Touch **m.**) *mmm.*
b. **(test item)** Point to the boxed **a.**) Let's see if you remember this sound. (Pause.) What sound? (Touch **a.**) *ăăă.*

Task 2   Total possible: 6 points

(Circle 1 point on the scoring sheet for each correct response at *b*, *c*, and *d*.)

a. I'll say a word slowly. Then I'll say it fast. Listen. (Pause.) **Mmmaaannn.** (Pause.) I can say it fast. **Man.**
b. **(test item)** Your turn. Say (pause) **iiinnn.** *iiinnn.* **(test item)** Say it fast. *In.*
c. **(test item)** Your turn. Say (pause) **aaat.** *Aaat.* **(test item)** Say it fast. *At.*
d. **(test item)** Your turn. Say (pause) **sssiiit.** *Sssiiit.* **(test item)** Say it fast. *Sit.*

End of Placement Test

Placement

For coordination of Reading and Language, see page 3. Before you begin teaching the program, administer the placement test on pages 8–9. to each child. Use the test to determine whether a child enters *Reading Mastery,* Grade K at lesson 1 or at lesson 11 or whether the child should enter *Reading Mastery: Fast Cycle.* The test is scored on the Placement Test Scoring Sheet, which appears on page 83 of this book. Make one copy of this sheet for each child.

Administer the test individually to each child, circling the number of points earned for each exercise on a Placement Test Scoring Sheet. Then circle the appropriate entry point for the child. Testing each child requires about two to four minutes. You should be able to complete the testing of all the children within one hour on the first day of school. Instruction should begin on the second day.

Summary of Placement Information

Part 1 of the Placement Test

Children who made 0–14 points begin with *Reading Mastery,* Grade K, lesson 1.

Children who made 15–18 points begin with *Reading Mastery,* Grade K, lesson 11.

Children who made 19–20 points should proceed with Part 2 of the placement test.

Part 2 of the Placement Test

Children who made 0–7 points begin with *Reading Mastery,* Grade K, lesson 11.

Children who made 8–10 points should be placed, if possible, in *Reading Mastery:* Fast Cycle.

Placement Test Scoring Sheet for *Reading Mastery*

Student's Name _____ Date _____

Circle 1 point or 2 points if the student answers correctly.

	Part 1				Part 2		
Task 1	step b	0	1 point	Task 1	step a	0	2 points
	step c	0	1 point		step b	0	2 points
Task 2	step b	0	1 point	Task 2	step b	0	1 point
		0	1 point			0	1 point
		0	1 point		step c	0	1 point
		0	1 point			0	1 point
		0	1 point		step d	0	1 point
	step d	0	1 point			0	1 point
		0	1 point		Total Points ☐		
		0	1 point				
		0	1 point				
		0	1 point				
Task 3	step b	0	2 points				
	step c	0	2 points				
Task 4	step b	0	2 points				
	step d	0	2 points				
	Total Points ☐						

Number of Points	Start At:
0-7	*Reading Mastery*, Grade K, Lesson 11
8-10	If possible, should be placed in *Reading Mastery:* Classic Edition, Fast Cycle.

Number of Points	Start At:
0-14	*Reading Mastery*, Grade K, Lesson 1
15-18	*Reading Mastery*, Grade K, Lesson 11 (Circle the lesson)
19-20	Continue testing in part 2, (Check box) ☐

Grouping

Here is a guide for grouping children according to their performance on the placement test:

1. Divide the class into no more than three groups.

2. Make the lowest-performing group the smallest. Ideally, there should be no more than five or six children in this group.

3. The highest-performing group should be the largest.

Testing Throughout the Year

Throughout the program, children are given mastery tests. The tests are short, generally test only one skill, and are given after specified lessons in the program. They are administered separately from the regular reading lesson.

There are thirty tests in all. They appear in the Presentation Books at the points at which they are to be presented. The first test is to be given after lesson 8; after that, a test is scheduled after every five lessons. There is a note at the end of each lesson that is to be followed by a test.

The mastery tests give you feedback on the effectiveness of your teaching; they serve as a backup for your daily evaluation of the children's performance; they provide criteria for skipping procedures, allowing more capable groups of children to move more rapidly through the program; and they provide information for regrouping the children at later points in the program.

Administering the Mastery Tests

Use the following procedures when administering the mastery tests.

1. Test each child individually.

2. No child should see or hear another child being tested before he or she has taken the test.

3. Test the children at a time other than the regularly scheduled reading lesson. Your most capable children may be tested a day or two early so that only the children you are doubtful about will have to be tested on the day indicated in the Presentation Book.

4. Before presenting a test, write the names of the children in the group on a sheet of paper. After presenting each test item, record a pass (P) or a fail (F) next to the child's name. At the end of the test, record the total number of items missed by the child.

5. When presenting the test, have the child sit next to you so that both of you can see and work from the test page.

6. Use the plastic page protector when doing the story-reading tests.

The children's performance on a test determines whether the group should skip a lesson, proceed to the next lesson, or repeat exercises from previous lessons in order to firm up a critical skill. The criterion for a weak group is specified at the end of each test. Procedures for firming critical skills are also provided. These firming procedures may take longer than a single reading period.

If a group is weak, present the firming procedures to the entire group, but readminister the test only to those children who failed it initially. If the group is still weak, review and practice the critical teaching behaviors that are discussed in the Teacher's Guide for the skill being tested. Then repeat the firming procedures and retest the group. If the group is considered firm but more than one child was weak on the test items, present the firming procedures to the children who were weak. Do the firming at a time other than the regularly scheduled reading lesson. Do not prevent the entire group from moving ahead to the next lesson.

Skipping

The program is designed so that higher-performing children can complete the entire program in 123 days, skipping a total of 37 lessons. The number of lessons that a group skips will be determined by their performance on the placement test and by their continuing performance on the mastery tests. All groups may skip some lessons if they do well on the tests. When the children skip a lesson, you may choose to have them complete the workbook exercises for the skipped lesson during a free period.

Regrouping

Any child who repeatedly fails items on the mastery tests should be placed in a lower reading group. Repeated failure indicates that the child cannot maintain the pace set by other members of the group. If a child is already in the lowest-performing group, try to work with the child individually. If there are several teachers using *Reading Mastery,* Grade K in your school, consider forming a group of these low performers and assigning them to one teacher. This will permit the children to receive the individual attention they need. It will also allow the groups from which they have been removed to progress at a faster rate.

On the other hand, a child who entered the program with few skills may learn quickly. If a child consistently performs better than most of the other children in the group, the child should be moved to a higher group. Plan to regroup the children at several points throughout the year. Suggested points for regrouping are after Mastery Test 4 (lesson 25), after Mastery Test 8 (lesson 45), and after Mastery Test 14 (lesson 75).

Group Performance

It is important to complete a lesson each day with each group, even with the lowest performers. When some new skills are introduced, however, you may find that if you firm the skill so that all children can perform, you will not be able to complete the entire lesson. When the choice is between firming all the children and completing the lesson, choose the firming. The best procedure is to firm the children when new skills are first introduced; however, the number of lessons that cannot be completed during the allotted time should be small compared to those that can be successfully completed (with all children firm on every exercise), particularly if you make sure that the children are firm early in the program.

There are 160 lessons in *Reading Mastery,* Grade K. Below are reasonable expectations for the performance of different groups of children. These expectations are based on a school year of 170 available teaching days.

Highest-performing groups	210 lessons
Middle-performing groups	170 lessons
Lowest-performing groups	120–130 lessons

Note that the highest-performing groups and the middle-performing groups should complete *Reading Mastery,* Grade K in less than a school year. Upon completion of the Grade K program, they should continue into *Reading Mastery,* Grade 1 until the end of the school year.

PRESENTING *READING MASTERY* EXERCISES

The remainder of this guide gives you first general, then specific, instructions on how to teach *Reading Mastery,* Grade K. Pages 13–16 specify general teaching strategies (how to seat the children, how to present signals so that children respond together, and so forth). Following the general teaching strategies is a detailed description of the prereading exercises and how to present them. Next is a section on reading. The last section explains the children's independent work.

Before teaching the program, study pages 17 to 32 and practice each of the formats included in the Teacher's Guide. Simply examining the exercises will not ensure that you present them well; you must actually say the words, practice the signals, and practice the various corrections that are specified. You will see that, when you begin working with children, they will make the mistakes indicated in the formats and that the corrections you practice will be needed.

Throughout the year, consult this Teacher's Guide for new formats that will be appearing in the program. Always practice new formats before the top group reaches them. In this way you will be reasonably well prepared for your top group, and by the time your lowest-performing group reaches the lesson on which the new format appears, you will be quite proficient at presenting it.

GENERAL TEACHING STRATEGIES

How to Set Up the Group

1. Seat the children in a semicircle in front of you. Sit so that you can observe every child in the group, as well as the other members of the class who are engaged in independent work. Children in the group should sit on chairs, not at desks.

2. Test to see that all children can see the Presentation Book. Do this by holding your head next to the book and looking to see whether you can see the eyes of all the children. If you have to look almost sideways from the book to see a child's eyes, that child won't be able to see what is on the page.

3. Keep all children within touching distance. There will be times during the lesson when you will want to hand the Presentation Book to a child, or touch a child to reinforce him or her. This will be easier if they are all within arm's reach of you. Sit close to the children and group them close together.

4. Place the lowest performers directly in front of you (in the first row if there is more than one row). Seat the highest performers on the ends of the group (or in the second row). You will naturally look most frequently at the children seated directly in front of you. You want to teach until each child is firm. If you are constantly looking at the lower performers, you will be in a position to know when they are firm. When the lowest performers are firm, the rest of the group will be firm.

5. Seat the children so that cliques are broken. Assign the seats. The children should sit in their assigned seats each day. This will allow you to separate disruptive buddies, and allow you to learn which voices to listen to during the presentation.

Getting into the Lesson

1. Introduce the rules that the group is to follow on the first day that you begin a lesson. Tell the children what they are expected to do. Summarize the rules: "Sit tall, look at the book, and talk big." Note that these rules express precisely what the children are supposed to do. Reinforce the children for following the rules.

2. Get into the lesson *quickly.* If the group is shy or tends to present behavior problems, begin by telling the children "Stand up . . . touch your nose . . ." until all of them are responding without hesitation. This activity gets the children responding and establishes you as directing what they are to do. Then quickly present the first exercise. The same technique can be used if the children's attention lags during the presentation. It will break the pace and again establish you as directing what the children are to do.

3. Present each exercise until the children are firm. If the first exercise is a Say It Fast exercise, do not move on to the second exercise in the lesson until all the children are firm. The best time to get them all responding together until firm is the first time the exercise is presented. This establishes what your criterion of performance is. Further information on teaching to criterion appears below.

4. Use clear signals. All signals have the same purpose: to trigger a simultaneous response from the group. All signals have the same rationale: if you can get the group to respond simultaneously (with no child leading the others) you will get information about the performance of all the children, not just those who happen to answer first.

   Practice the specific signal for each new exercise before practicing the rest of the exercise. Practice the signals until they are natural and you can do them without concentrating on them. The execution of a clear, easy-to-follow signal will result in efficient teaching of all the exercises.

5. Pace exercises appropriately. Pacing is one of the more difficult presentational skills to master. Pacing is the rate at which different parts of the exercise are presented. All portions of a exercise should not be presented at the same rate.

   Different pacing is specified throughout the guide. Many of the formats contain such instructions as "pause one second," or "pause three seconds." Note that all signals are paced with the same timing. The children learn that the signal will follow one second after you stop talking in an exercise. Keep this interval constant.

6. Reinforce the children's good performance. Make your praise specific. If the children are working hard on a difficult skill, tell them so. "You are working hard and this is tough. Keep at it—you'll get it." If they just completed a Sounds page with no errors, reinforce them, "Wow! You know every sound on the page." If they have just said the sounds in *am* correctly, say "Yes, **am**." Repeating the children's correct response is very reinforcing.

   Praise them for following the rules within the group. If they are all talking up, say, "Good talking. I can hear everybody." Catch the children in the act of being good and reinforce them for responding correctly.

   Early in the program, some of your lower-performing groups may not respond to verbal praise. These children may need more tangible rewards. Do not assume, however, that the children need tangible rewards. Reinforce them first with verbal praise and a handshake or a pat on the back. If they do not respond to this kind of praise, find something that works—stickers, raisins, or points accumulated toward a small reward. Remember, you have to find something that they like—something that they are willing to work for. If you have to use tangible rewards, always tell the children why they are receiving a star or a raisin. Say "Good talking big, Mary," as you hand Mary a raisin.

Teaching to Criterion

At the conclusion of any exercise every child should be able to perform the exercise independently, without any need for corrections. Children are "at criterion" or "firm" on a exercise only when they can perform quickly and confidently with the correct response. Your goal is to teach so that every child is at criterion.

It is easier to bring the children to criterion on the first introduction of a format than it will be at a later time in the program, because they haven't performed the exercise incorrectly many times or heard others performing it incorrectly.

The initial formats in each track include a demonstration by you of the response that the children are to make. This allows the children to hear the correct response the first time that the exercise is presented.

Let the children know what your criterion is. Keep on a exercise until you can honestly say to them, "Terrific. Everybody read every word correctly." The stricter your criterion, the fewer the exercises your group will have to repeat after taking the mastery tests.

Individual Turns

Individual turns are specified in the exercises or under the heading *Individual Test*. There are several rules to follow when administering individual turns:

1. Present individual turns only after the group is firm. If you go to individual turns too soon, many of the children will not be able to give a firm response. If you wait until the children are firm on group responses, the chances are much better that each will be able to give a firm response on an individual turn.

2. Give most of your individual turns to the lower-performing children in the group—those children seated directly in front of you. By watching these children during the group practice of the exercise, you can tell when they are ready to perform individually. When these children can perform the exercise without further need of correction, you can safely assume that the other children in the group will be able to perform the task.

3. Individual turns are not specified in all exercises. If you are in doubt about the performance of any children on these exercises, present quick individual turns. Always include the individual turns for exercises in which they are specified.

4. The following procedure is recommended for administering individual turns once the group responses on an exercise are firm. First you can state: "Time for individual turns." Then <u>focus</u> on the task for the students to practice. Finally, call on an individual student to respond to the task. This procedure helps to keep the entire group alert to you and practicing the exercise until a specific student's name is called.

Corrections

The major difference between the average *Reading Mastery,* Grade K teacher, who teaches <u>most</u> of the children, and the outstanding teacher, who teaches <u>all</u> of the children, is the ability to correct.

Information on general corrections appears below. Information on specific corrections is included with the discussions of individual exercises later in this guide. Study the procedures and practice them until you can execute them immediately, without hesitation. Corrections must be automatic. Failure to get each child to pay attention or allowing part of the group not to respond will result in some of the children not learning.

Unacceptable behavior that calls for correction includes nonattending, nonresponding, signal violations, and response errors.

1. *Nonattending.* This behavior occurs when a child is not looking where he or she should be looking during a exercise. For example, if a child is not attending to the sound to which you are pointing, correct by looking at the nonattender and saying:

Watch my finger.
Let's try it again.
Return to the beginning of the exercise.

Reinforce the children who are paying attention. Let them know you are watching all of them all the time. Always return to the beginning of the exercise to enforce your rule that everyone has to pay attention at all times.

2. *Nonresponding.* This behavior occurs when a child fails to answer when you signal a response. It is dangerous to overlook nonresponding. The children may learn to just listen the first time an exercise is presented and then join in later. They will learn dependence on other children and get the idea that they need not answer along with the rest of the group. If a child is not responding, correct the child by saying:

I have to hear everybody.
Return to the beginning of the exercise.

Failure to return to the beginning of the exercise will teach the children that you really do not mean that you "have to hear everybody." It is very important to enforce this rule from the first day of instruction so that the children learn you are expecting everyone to perform on every exercise.

3. *Signal Violations.* A signal violation occurs when the child responds either before or too long after the signal, or during the portion of the exercise in which you are demonstrating. For example, a child might begin to say a sound after you have touched it and after the other children respond. The lower-performing children are most likely to violate the signal, because they will tend to wait for the higher-performing children in a group to respond first.

If children respond either early or late, you will not get information from every child. Remember that the purpose of a signal is to trigger a simultaneous group response. If you fail to enforce the signal, you will have to resort to a great many individual turns to find out which children are firm and which children are weak.

Correct signal-violation mistakes in Sounds, for example, by telling the children what they did, repeating the signal, and then returning to the beginning of the exercise:

You're early, or You're late, or You didn't say it when I touched it, or I stopped touching it, but you kept saying it.
Watch my finger. Get ready. Touch.
Children respond as you touch.
Now, let's try it again.
Return to the beginning of the exercise.

Only if you consistently return to the beginning of the exercise after each signal-violation correction will the children learn to attend to your signal. Once they learn that you will repeat the exercise until they are all responding on signal, they will attend much more closely to the signal.

If you find that you are spending a lot of time correcting nonattending, nonresponding, and signal violations, your pacing is probably too slow, or your pacing of the signal inconsistent. The object of a signal is not to keep the children sitting on the edges of their seats, never knowing when they will have to respond next. The pacing of the signal should be perfectly predictable.

4. *Response Errors.* A response error is any response inconsistent with the one called for in the exercise. If you are teaching sounds, and the children say *mmm* when you touch under **a,** this is a response error. They may have followed your signal and said the sound just when you touched under it, but their response is inconsistent with the symbol you are pointing to.

Response errors are specific to the individual exercise. The correction for each response error, therefore, must be specific. The children's mistakes can be anticipated. Many of the corrections that will be most often required appear on the page with the appropriate format in the Presentation Book. The most common mistakes that children make are also identified, and the appropriate correction supplied, in the discussion of specific formats in the Prereading Skills and Reading sections of this guide. It is very important to practice these corrections. You must be able to present the correction without hesitation when the mistake occurs. By practicing the corrections, you will be well prepared for the common mistakes that the children will make.

The first formats in almost every track are written so that you first demonstrate, or model, the response the children are to make. Frequently the next step is a teacher lead, in which you respond with the children. Leading is a very powerful technique. It gives the children the benefit of responding with you until they are confident in the response they are to make. Many exercises require a number of teacher leads before the children are producing firm responses. The lead is a correction. Don't be afraid to continue leading until the children are producing the response with you. Following the teacher lead, present a test in which the children produce the response on their own. The final step in any correction is a delayed test. Go back to an earlier step in the exercise and present the steps in sequence. If the children respond correctly and firmly, the correction has been effective.

A useful way to think of all kinds of corrections is that they provide the child with the kind of practice needed to pass a test. The exercise that you present is a test. When the child makes a mistake, he or she fails the test. The child needs help. You can help by modeling, showing the child what to do. You may be able to help further by leading. When the child is firm, readminister the test. If the correction worked, the child will pass the test.

PREREADING SKILLS

At lesson 28 the children begin to read words. Lessons 1 to 27 are designed to set the stage for the word reading. The activities presented in this part of the program are possibly the most important in the entire program. If children master these activities, they typically have little trouble with the next instructional steps. However, if children are not taught these important prereading skills, they will probably have serious trouble throughout the program.

During these beginning lessons, children learn to identify symbols as "sounds"; they practice sequencing events—*first* and *next* events; they firm their oral-blending skills by saying words slowly and saying them fast; and they learn to rhyme. Rhyming provides a basis for seeing how words may be divided into families based on their ending sounds.

GENERAL TEACHING STRATEGIES

To teach successfully, you must be able to communicate clearly with the children and receive clear information on what they understand or the specific problems they are experiencing. Success in communicating implies that you give the group clear signals about when to respond; that you present the formats or activities in the program so they are well paced; that you respond quickly to mistakes by presenting the appropriate correction procedure; and that you present individual turns so that you can carefully evaluate the performance of each child.

The following section of this guide is designed to help you practice the specific skills that you will use when working with children. The section explains the purpose of each track in the prereading section. It presents some of the key formats or exercises within the track. It also indicates how to correct some of the more common mistakes the children will make.

The best way to learn the skills that are required is to practice, and the best way to practice is with a partner. During the initial practice sessions, you and your partner should take turns playing the roles of teacher and child. The "child" should respond correctly to all exercises and should give the "teacher" feedback about how the teacher executed the different parts of the format.

Mastering Signals

A signal shows each child when to respond so that each will originate an independent response and yet all children will respond together. The signal or signals used in each track are described before specific formats are discussed, and should be learned through practice before you review the formats. If you learn these signals well, you will be prepared to execute the motor behaviors for any of the formats.

Here are a few suggestions for studying and practicing the prereading formats.

- Learn to execute the signal or signals smoothly and automatically.
- Read the format.
- Review the teaching techniques.
- Rehearse the pacing of the key statements you are to make.
- Combine the script of the format with the signals.
- Practice the entire format, repeating it several times.
- Practice the format again, until you can perform it confidently.

After you are able to run the format smoothly, practice the format with corrections. Practice correcting mistakes the children are most likely to make. Anticipate that you will have to use each of these corrections. Facility in executing the corrections will make a great deal of difference in the performance of the children, especially those in your lowest-performing group.

Memorize the steps in the corrections. Continue to practice the corrections until you can respond automatically to any mistake with the appropriate correction. As soon as the error is made, go immediately into the correction, then return quickly to the appropriate step in the format.

In *Reading Mastery,* Grade K, students are initially taught to decode words by sounding them out. To sound out a word successfully students must be firm in sounds identification. Sounds activities, therefore, appear in every lesson in the program. The two primary formats in the Sounds track are a *sound introduction* format, used to introduce and reinforce each new sound, and a *sound firming* format, in which several sounds are reviewed and firmed up. Other formats include game formats such as a cross-out game, a child-plays-teacher game, and a sounds game.

Letters are referred to as *sounds* in *Reading Mastery,* Grade K. Alphabet names are taught in *Reading Mastery,* Grade 1.

Throughout most of *Reading Mastery,* Grade K, each symbol stands for a single sound. The symbol **a** stands for the sound *aaa* (as in *and*). It does not stand for **a** as in **ate,** in **all,** or in **father.**

To allow the children to read more words as "regular words" four conventions are followed in the program:

1. Several sounds are represented by joined letters: *th, ch, sh, wh, qu, er, oo,* and *ing.*
2. Macrons (long lines over vowels) differentiate long vowels from short vowels. For example, the symbol **ā** makes the long vowel sound in **āte.**
3. Some symbols are altered to reduce some of the confusion children typically have between pairs of letters that appear very much alike in traditional orthography. For example:

b d   h n   f t   j i

4. Only lowercase letters are taught in *Reading Mastery,* Grade K so that the children will not have to learn two symbols for each sound.

By the middle of *Reading Mastery,* Grade 1, all letters are printed in traditional orthography. The capital letters are taught in *Reading Mastery,* Grade 1.

The children are taught forty sounds. Initially only one value is taught for each sound. New sounds are introduced about every three to four lessons. A list of the lessons in which new sounds are introduced is included in the pronunciation chart on the inside back cover of this guide. The first three sounds are introduced twice so that students entering the program at lesson 1 receive extra practice on these three sounds. Note that children start to read words at lesson 28, after six sounds have been introduced.

The first five sounds are *a, m, s, ē,* and *r.* Before teaching the program, practice pronouncing the sounds that appear on the pronunciation chart on the inside back cover of this guide. The compact disc that accompanies this program models the correct pronunciation of all forty sounds. (Track 1)

Note that some sounds are continuous sounds and some are stop sounds. Continuous sounds can be held until you run out of breath. Continuous sounds include all vowels and such consonants and digraphs as *s, m, r, l, th,* and *sh.* Stop sounds are sounds that must be produced very quickly, like *d, b, c, g, h, p, t.*

The first sounds in the program are continuous sounds because they are easier for the children to pronounce.

Continuous Sound Signal

All signals follow the same basic rules:
- You talk first, then signal.
- You never signal when talking.
- You always pause the same length of time between the <u>end</u> of your talking and the signal for the children to respond, about one second.

Remember, talk first, then signal, and keep the timing the same for every signal.

You use signals to permit a group of children to respond together with every child in the group initiating the response, not merely imitating what others in the group do. Therefore, your signal must be very clear and easy to follow. Think of a signal as something like a dance step. If it's done right, and in time, your partner can follow. If the timing is off, somebody's going to stumble.

To signal children to respond to a continuous sound, follow these steps:

- Touch the first ball of the arrow.
- Keep your finger on that ball as you say, "Get ready."
- Pause for one second. Then move quickly to the ball under **a** and hold on that ball for two seconds. As soon as you touch that ball, <u>all</u> the children are to respond.

Practice touching the first ball, saying, "Get ready," pausing one second, then moving quickly to the second ball and holding your finger there for two seconds.

Continuous Sounds Teaching Techniques

Practice the following sounds-introduction format from lesson 1 after you are very consistent with your signal. Note that the last thing you say before signaling is always, "Get ready." Timing is the same as it is for the simple signal that you practiced. Pause after saying "Get ready" and move quickly to the second ball. Hold at the second ball as either you or the children respond. The letters **aaa** in the teacher's script remind you to hold the sound.

EXERCISE 4

Introducing the new sound **aaa** as in **and**

Track 2

a. (Touch the first ball of the arrow.) Here's a new sound. My turn to say it. When I move under the sound, I'll say it. I'll keep on saying it as long as I touch under it. Get ready. (Move quickly to the second ball of the arrow. Hold for two seconds.) **aaa.**

b. (Touch the first ball of the arrow.) My turn again. Get ready. (Move quickly to the second ball of the arrow. Hold for two seconds.) **aaa.**

c. (Touch the first ball of the arrow.) My turn again. Get ready. (Move quickly to the second ball of the arrow. Hold for two seconds.) **aaa.**

d. (Touch the first ball of the arrow.) Your turn. When I move under the sound, you say it. Keep on saying it as long as I touch under it. Get ready. (Move quickly to the second ball of the arrow. Hold for two seconds.) *aaa.* Yes, **aaa.**

To Correct
(If the children do not say *aaa*:)
model — 1. **aaa.**
lead — 2. (Touch the first ball of the arrow.) Say it with me. Get ready. (Move quickly to the second ball of the arrow. Hold for two seconds. Say aaa with the children.) *aaa.*
test — 3. (Touch the first ball of the arrow.) Your turn. Get ready. (Move quickly to the second ball of the arrow. Hold for two seconds.) *aaa.*

e. (Touch the first ball of the arrow.) Again. Get ready. (Move quickly to the second ball of the arrow. Hold for two seconds.) *aaa.* Yes, **aaa.**

f. (Repeat e until firm.)

g. (Call on individual children to do d.)

h. Good saying **aaa.**

- Steps a to c model the behavior so the children know what they should respond and how they should respond in steps d and e.
- Step d is the first time the students are to respond.
- Following step d is a correction to be used if the children respond incorrectly. Present the correction <u>as soon as</u> you hear or see any child responding incorrectly. The correction steps have been labeled to help you see the model-lead-test procedure.
- Step f directs you to repeat step e until firm. "Firm" means that all children are responding clearly as soon as you touch under the sound and that all children are saying the sound as long as you touch under it.

- At step *g* you call on individual children to identify the sound. Remember to include lower-performing children in your individual turns. If a child makes a mistake on step *g*, <u>present the correction to the group</u>, then repeat steps *e* through *g*.

Stop-Sound Signal

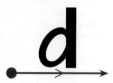

The sound *d* above is a stop sound, a sound that cannot be held for more than an instant without distorting it.

The following procedures are used to signal for stop sounds:
- Touch the first ball of the arrow.
- Say "Say it fast."
- Pause for one second.
- Quickly move your finger to the end of the arrow. As you pass under the arrowhead that is directly under the **d**, the children are to say the sound, *d* (not *duh* or *dih*, simply *d*).

Note that the signal for the stop sound involves the same timing as the signal for the continuous sound. The only difference is that you don't stop under the sound; you just keep moving to the end of the arrow.

If you have trouble pronouncing a stop sound, say a word that ends in the sound. Say the sound in an exaggerated manner. That is the way you would pronounce it when teaching children to identify the symbol. For instance, say the word **sad,** exaggerating the **d.** Be careful not to say *saduh.*

Stop Sounds Teaching Techniques

In the teacher's script and on the pronunciation guide, stop sounds are represented by a single letter such as **d, t,** or **c,** to help you remember to say the sound fast. This compares with the three letters (**aaa**) used to remind you to hold continuous sounds. After practicing the basic signal for stop sounds, practice the following sounds-introduction format.

Lesson 27

EXERCISE 2

Introducing the new sound **d** as in **dad**

a. (Touch the ball of the arrow for **d.**) We always have to say this sound fast. The little arrow under the sound tells me that I can't stop under this sound. My turn to say it fast. (Slash to the end of the arrow as you say d.) (Return to the ball.) My turn to say it fast again. (Slash to the end of the arrow as you say d.)

b. (Touch the ball of the arrow.) Your turn. Say it fast. (Slash to the end of the arrow.) d. Yes, **d.**

c. (Repeat *b* until firm.)

d. (Call on individual children to do *b*.)

d

In step *b*, pause after you say "Your turn," and before you say "Say it fast," to give the children a moment to think.

Corrections

If students mispronounce the sound at step *b*, correct as follows:

model ⟶ **1.** Say d.
test ⟶ **2.** Touch the ball of the arrow.
Say Your turn. Say it fast.
Slash to the end of the arrow.
Children say *d*.

Sounds Firm-up Teaching Techniques

In sounds firm-up exercises children review and practice the sounds they have learned. Sounds firm-up exercises appear in every lesson starting with lesson 5. Firm-up exercises are the most important source of feedback about how well children have learned sounds. There are no new signals in the exercise. Use the signals for a continuous sound and for a stop sound that you have already practiced.

Lesson 27   Track 7

EXERCISE 3

Sounds firm-up

a. (Point to the sounds in the columns.) Get ready to tell me all these sounds. Remember, if a sound has a little arrow under it, you have to say it fast. Don't get fooled.

b. (Touch the first ball of the arrow for **r.** Pause one second.) Get ready. (Move quickly to the second ball. Hold.) *rrr.* Yes, **rrr.**

c. (Repeat b for each remaining sound. For **d,** slash to the end of the arrow.)

d. (Repeat b and c until all children are firm on all sounds.)

e. (Call on individual children to say all the sounds.)

f. Good. You said all the sounds.

r →

e →

d →

Step *e* of the format calls for individual children to say all the sounds in the column. The individual test is very important. You will receive feedback about how well each child has learned the sounds. Make sure that you give turns to the lower-performing children.

Corrections

No correction box is in the exercise. If any child in the group misidentifies the sound at step *b,* correct as follows:

model ⟶ **1.** Say rrr.

test ⟶ **2.** Touch the first ball of the arrow for **r.**
Pause one second. Say Everybody, get ready. Move to the second ball.
Hold. Children say: *rrr.*

The following dialogue illustrates how to handle mistakes on individual turns. The teacher presents an individual turn to Lucy, who makes a mistake at step 4. The teacher corrects the group, then returns to Lucy. This procedure is important. If an individual child makes a mistake, assume that others in the group would make the same mistake. By first correcting the group, you save time, because you won't have to present the same correction to other members of the group.

Read the dialogue out loud. Make sure that you understand why the teacher takes each of the steps that appears in the script.

Script for Step e

1. Teacher: (Touch the first ball of the arrow for **r.**) Lucy, your turn to say all the sounds in this column. (Pause one second.) Get ready. (Move quickly to the second ball. Hold.)
2. Lucy: *rrr.*
3. Teacher: Yes, **rrr.** (Touch the first ball of the arrow for **ē.**) (Pause one second.) Get ready. (Move quickly to the second ball. Hold.)
4. Lucy: *aaa.*
5. Teacher: **ēēē.** (Return to the first ball of the arrow for **ē.** Pause one second.) Everybody, get ready. (Move quickly to the second ball. Hold.)
6. Group: *ēēē.*
7. Teacher: Yes, **ēēē.** (Return to the first ball of the arrow for **ē.** Pause one second.) Lucy, get ready. (Move quickly to the second ball. Hold.)
8. Lucy: *ēēē.*
9. Teacher: Yes, **ēēē.** (Return to the top of the column. Touch the first ball of the arrow for **r.**) Starting over. (Pause one second.) Lucy, get ready. (Move quickly to the second ball. Hold.)
10. Lucy: *rrr.*
11. Teacher: Yes, **rrr.** (Touch the first ball of the arrow for **ē.** Pause one second.) Get ready. (Move quickly to the second ball. Hold.)
12. Lucy: *ēēē.*
13. Teacher: Yes, **ēēē.** (Touch the ball of the arrow for **d.** Pause one second.) Get ready. (Slash to the end of the arrow.)
14. Lucy: *d.*
15. Teacher: Yes, **d.** Good. You said all the sounds in the column.

Purpose of the Track

This track provides practice in pronouncing sounds. All Pronunciation exercises are oral. The children practice saying a sound before they identify the written symbol for that sound. The sounds that are practiced include those that may be difficult to pronounce. Pronunciation exercises precede Sounds exercises, and always include any new sounds that will be introduced in that lesson.

Pronunciation Signal

To signal a sound response, hold up one finger. This signal will be used in several other tracks, including those oral tracks in which students say words or word parts slowly.

Lesson 2

EXERCISE 1

Children say the sounds

a. You're going to say some sounds. When I hold up my finger, say (pause) **ăăă.** Get ready. (Hold up one finger.) **ăăă.**

b. Next sound. Say (pause) **mmm.** Get ready. (Hold up one finger.) *mmm.*

c. Next sound. Say (pause) **d.** Get ready. (Hold up one finger.) *d.*

d. (Repeat c for sounds **ăăă, mmm,** and **d.**)

e. (Call on individual children to do *a, b,* or *c.*)

f. Good saying the sounds.

Note that only in this oral exercise are short vowels written as ăăă or ŏŏŏ.

Pronunciation Teaching Techniques

- Signal so that continuous sounds like *aaa* or *mmm* are held for about two seconds, and stop sounds such as *d* are said fast.
- Make sure that children are pronouncing sounds correctly.
- When presenting a sound, remember to pause when saying Say (pause) **ăăă.**
- Remember to present step *c* for each sound.

Corrections

Correct mistakes by presenting a lead, then a test.

lead ⟶ **1.** (Say) Say it with me. Get ready. (Hold up one finger.) *aaa.* Again. Get ready. (Hold up one finger.) *aaa.*

test ⟶ **2.** Your turn. Get ready. (Hold up one finger.) *The students say aaa.*

SYMBOL ACTION
(Lessons 1–17)

The Symbol Action games give the children practice in using the same "code" for sequencing events that they use in reading words. Written words contain letters that stand for sounds. The sounds are to be produced in order, from left to right.

The Symbol Action games present the same left-to-right code. The difference is that the events to be sequenced are not letters or sounds, but actions that are pictured on an arrow.

The Symbol Action games teach students to respond to the words first and next. These words will be used on worksheet activities, in sequencing word parts, in sounding-out, in word-reading, and in sentence-reading.

The Symbol Action games are highly reinforcing to the children and easy for you to correct. They use the same starting ball, balls under the pictures, and arrows that will later appear when word reading is introduced.

Before lesson 13, the children practice performing the one or two actions pictured on the arrow. In the next several lessons they perform the actions you refer to as first and next.

Children must remember what to do first and next before they do it. They then perform the actions without looking at the pictures.

EXERCISE 3

Children do **first** and **next**

a. (Touch the first ball of the arrow.) First you'll do what it shows on the arrow. Then we'll see if you can do it without looking at the picture. My turn. Watch. (Move quickly to the second ball and stop.) This is what you do first. (Touch your ear.) Show me what you do first. (Tap the second ball.) *Children touch their ear with either hand.*

• Watch. (Move quickly to the third ball and stop.) This is what you do next. (Touch your nose.) Show me what you do next. (Tap the third ball.) *Children touch their nose.*

b. (Touch the first ball of the arrow.) Let's do it again. Show me what you're going to do first. (Move quickly to the second ball and stop.) *Children touch their ear with either hand.*

• Show me what you're going to do next. (Move quickly to the third ball and stop.) *Children touch their nose.*

c. (Repeat *b* until firm.)

d. (Do not show the pictures.) Let's see if you remember what you did first and what you did next. Show me what you did first. Get ready. (Signal.) *Children touch their ear with either hand.*

• Show me what you did next. Get ready. (Signal.) *Children touch their nose.*

e. (Repeat *d* until firm.)

f. (Call on individual children to do *d.*)

• Practice step *a* several times. You will need to coordinate saying your lines with the various motor activities called for. Place the book on a table or use the teacher box as an easel. This makes it possible for you to use both hands.

• At step *b,* tap the ball under the picture to signal the children to respond.

• At steps *d* and *f,* turn the book so that the children cannot see the page. To signal, hold up a finger or use a hand-drop signal. (See page 24.)

Corrections

If children make a mistake at step *a,* model. Touch under the appropriate ball of the arrow. This is what you do **first**. Touch your head. Show me what you do **first**. Tap the ball. Or, This is what you do **next**. Open your mouth. Show me what you do **next**. Tap the ball.

Children should not have difficulties at steps *d* and *f* if you repeat step *b* until they are firm.

BLENDING

Children start to read words, such as **mē** and **am,** in lesson 28. The initial strategy the children are taught is to first sound out the word, then say it fast. This operation involves many skills. Children must be able to identify the symbols in the word. Children must understand that the written word presents a left-to-right code for sequencing the sounds. Finally, children must be able to say the sounds of the word slowly and then say the sounds fast. These skills—saying words slowly and saying them fast—are blending skills. When we remove them from the context of word reading, they are oral activities.

Oral-blending activities begin in lesson 1 and continue through the Prereading lessons. The first blending activity is Say It Fast, which is followed by activities in which children say words slowly.

SAY IT FAST (Lessons 1–24)

To introduce the children to blending in easy stages, you start by presenting long words broken into two parts—words like **motor** (pause) **boat** and **ham** (pause) **burger.** In later lessons you say the sounds of one-syllable words without pausing between the sounds: *aaammm* and *sssēēē*. Many of the short words that the children say fast are words that they will read in the early Reading Vocabulary lessons. This initial oral practice allows them to concentrate on listening to the sounds and saying the word without interference from written symbols. Frequently, pictures will be shown to the children after they have responded successfully. The pictures relate to the word and serve as reinforcers for saying the word fast.

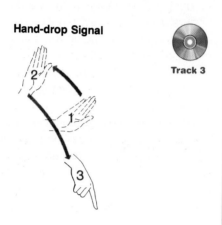

Hand-drop Signal

Track 3

Say It Fast Signal

The key words in the Say It Fast signal are "Hold out your hand" and "Drop your hand."

- Hold out your hand as if you were stopping traffic.
- Keep it perfectly still.
- After saying Say it fast, wait one second, then pull your hand up slightly and drop it quickly.
- The interval between "Say it fast" and the hand drop must be one second.

Say It Fast Teaching Techniques

Following is the basic Say It Fast format. It is simple and easy to learn after you have mastered the signal.

- In step *b,* hold your hand steady until after you have said, Say it fast.
- Say the word slowly in a monotone, without inflection.
- The children should respond as soon as your hand drops.
- Always repeat the word (Yes, **me.**) to reinforce the correct response.
- Reinforce the children after they have responded correctly by saying, Good. You said it fast.

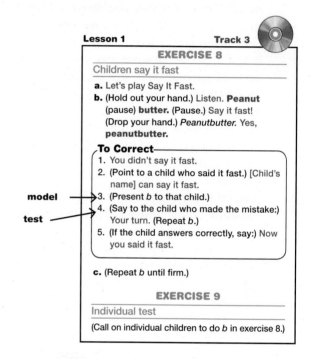

Lesson 1   Track 3

EXERCISE 8

Children say it fast

a. Let's play Say It Fast.
b. (Hold out your hand.) Listen. **Peanut** (pause) **butter.** (Pause.) Say it fast! (Drop your hand.) *Peanutbutter.* Yes, **peanutbutter.**

To Correct
1. You didn't say it fast.
2. (Point to a child who said it fast.) [Child's name] can say it fast.
3. (Present *b* to that child.) ← **model**
4. (Say to the child who made the mistake:) Your turn. (Repeat *b.*) ← **test**
5. (If the child answers correctly, say:) Now you said it fast.

c. (Repeat *b* until firm.)

EXERCISE 9

Individual test

(Call on individual children to do *b* in exercise 8.)

Corrections

If a child does not say the word fast, follow the correction in the format. Typically, the lower-performing children will not say the word fast at first. The correction is to tell the child what he or she did wrong, have another child model the correct response to the signal, and then test the child who made the mistake to see whether the child can respond correctly.

If a child says the wrong word fast, correct by saying, You said the wrong word. Let's try it again. Hold out your hand and repeat the correct word slowly.

Other Say It Fast Formats

Although there is only one basic Say It Fast format, your technique is somewhat different when you teach one-syllable words. When saying **ran** or **me,** say each sound slowly, without pausing between the sounds. You will need to practice this technique. A good way to tell whether you are saying the sounds without stopping between them is to say the word *man* very slowly with your hand on your throat. If you are saying the sounds without stopping, you will feel a constant vibration of your throat as you say the word.

Lesson 5

```
EXERCISE 10

Children say the words fast

a. Let's play Say It Fast.
b. (Hold out your hand.) Listen. Rrraaannn.
   Say it fast. (Drop your hand.) Ran. Yes, ran.
c. New word. (Hold out your hand.) Listen.
   Mmmēēē. Say it fast. (Drop your hand.)
   Me. Yes, me.
d. (Repeat b and c until firm.)
e. (Call on individual children to do b or c.)
```

SAY THE SOUNDS (Lesson 6–14)

Activities in this track provide practice in <u>oral</u> sounding out. Children do not say the words fast.

Say the Sounds Signal

The signal for any sound said slowly is the same as you practiced in the Pronunciation track. You hold up one finger for the **m** in *mmmēēē,* and a second finger for the **ē** in *mmmēēē.* Practice saying *mmmēēē,* holding up a finger for each sound.

To help you hold each continuous sound for two seconds, you may want to tap your foot two beats for each sound.

The activity below is from the first Say the Sounds format in the program.

- Before practicing step *a,* say the sounds *mmmēēē* without stopping between the sounds. Be sure that your voice is firm and that you hold each sound for two seconds.
- Now say the sounds *rrraaannn* and *nnnōōō.* Make sure that you are not pausing between the sounds. To test for a pause, hold your hand against your throat as you say *mmmēēē,* You should feel constant vibration in the throat. If the vibrations stop between the sounds *mmm* and *ēēē,* you paused. Practice until you can consistently say the words without pausing.

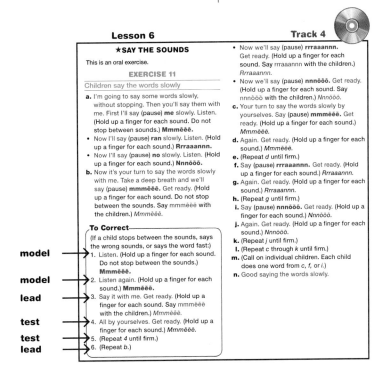

Corrections

The correction steps have been labeled to help you see the model-lead-test procedure.

Practice steps a and b with an adult partner. At step b, your partner makes any of the following errors: stops between the sounds (mmm . . . ēēē), says the wrong sounds (nnnēēē), or says the word fast (mē). Correct your partner using steps 1 through 6 of the correction. Note that step 5 tells you to repeat step 4—the test—until the "child" is firm. Step 6 sends you back to step b in the task.

Practice the correction with your partner making each of the mistakes listed above. Practice the correction until you feel firm.

Some children need considerable practice before they are able to say words slowly without stopping between the sounds. The program provides this practice, so don't be overly concerned if a child needs several lessons to master this skill. Correct the group and give the child several turns each day. Praise the child for trying hard.

Some children pronounce sounds inarticulately. Their pronunciation will improve, but the improvement is gradual. Praise a child whose pronunciation is improving. *You are really learning to say those sounds. I like it when you watch my mouth.*

SAY THE SOUNDS—SAY IT FAST
(Lessons 8–40)

This track consolidates the skills of saying words fast (taught in the Say It Fast track) and saying words slowly (taught in the Say the Sounds track).

Say the Sounds—Say It Fast Signals

Use two signals that you have already practiced—holding up one finger for each sound then dropping your hand to signal say it fast.

Practice steps a through f with another adult making no mistakes.

EXERCISE 11

Children say the word slowly, then say it fast

a. First you're going to say a word slowly without stopping between the sounds. Then you're going to say the word fast.

b. Listen. (Hold up a finger for each sound.) Say (pause) **mmmēēē.** Get ready. (Hold up a finger for each sound.) *Mmmēēē.*

• Again. Get ready. (Hold up a finger for each sound.) *Mmmēēē.*

• Say it fast. (Signal.) *Me.* Yes, **me.**

c. Listen. (Hold up a finger for each sound.) Say (pause) **rrraaannn.** Get ready. (Hold up a finger for each sound.) *Rrraaannn.*

• Again. Get ready. (Hold up a finger for each sound.) *Rrraaannn.*

• Say it fast. (Signal.) *Ran.* Yes, **ran.**

d. Listen. (Hold up a finger for each sound.) Say (pause) **ooonnn.** Get ready. (Hold up a finger for each sound.) *Ooonnn.*

• Again. Get ready. (Hold up a finger for each sound.) *Ooonnn.*

• Say it fast. (Signal.) *On.* Yes, **on.**

e. (Repeat b through d until firm.)

f. (Call on individual children to do b, c, or d.)

Correction

Use the same correction as you practiced in the Say the Sounds tasks—model, lead, and test. See page 25.

SOUNDS—SAY IT FAST
(Lessons 13–26)

When children sound out words, they first say the parts slowly, then say them fast. A simple variation of this procedure is to say a single sound slowly and then say it fast. For the exercises in this track, children respond to written symbols.

Sounds—Say It Fast Signals

In the Sounds track you practiced two signals, one signal for saying a sound slowly (mmm or aaa) and one signal for saying a sound fast (d). (See pages 19 and 20.) You will use both these signals in steps a and b of this format as you model how to say a sound slowly, then say it fast.

Sounds—Say It Fast Teaching Techniques

Practice steps *a* and *b*. Remember to return to the ball for the sound before you slash along the arrow to say it fast.

Steps *c* through *g* are tests in which the children first say a sound slowly, then say the same sound fast.

Practice steps *a* through *g* with your partner making no mistakes.

Lesson 13

EXERCISE 9

Children say a sound slowly, then say it fast

a. (Touch the first ball of the arrow for **m.**) First we're going to say this sound slowly. Then we're going to say it fast. My turn to say it slowly. Get ready. (Move quickly to the second ball. Hold for two seconds.) *mmmmmm.* (Return to the first ball.) My turn to say it fast. (Slash to the end of the arrow.) **m.**

b. (Touch the first ball of the arrow for **a.**) My turn to say it slowly. Get ready. (Move quickly to the second ball. Hold for two seconds.) *aaaaaa.* (Return to the first ball.) My turn to say it fast. (Slash to the end of the arrow.) **a.**

c. (Touch the first ball of the arrow for **m.**) Your turn. Say the sound slowly. Get ready. (Move quickly to the second ball. Hold for two seconds.) *mmmmmm.*

• (Return to the first ball.) Say it fast. (Slash to the end of the arrow.) *m.* Yes, **m.**

d. (Repeat *c* until firm.)

e. (Touch the first ball of the arrow for **a.**) Say the sound slowly. Get ready. (Move quickly to the second ball. Hold for two seconds.) *aaaaaa.*

• (Return to the first ball.) Say it fast. (Slash to the end of the arrow.) *a.* Yes, **a.**

f. (Repeat *e* until firm.)

g. (Call on individual children to do *c* or *e*.)

Correction

If a child makes a mistake, present a model (step *a* or *b*) to the group, then test the group or child.

RHYMING (Lessons 16–38)

There are two rhyming tracks. The first, called Say It Fast—Rhyming, contains activities that are verbal (with no written symbols). The second, called Rhyming, contains activities that involve written symbols. The activities in both tracks are similar. The children are either told or shown a beginning sound. They are also told the ending sound (or the "word" they're to rhyme with). The children then combine the sounds to create a word that they pronounce slowly (*mmmȳȳȳ*). Then they say it fast (*My*).

The verbal exercises appear first in the program (lessons 16 to 26). The exercises that involve symbols appear later (lessons 26 to 38).

At lesson 16, the children are first shown how to say a word slowly.

★SAY IT FAST—RHYMING
EXERCISE 10

Children say word parts slowly

a. My turn to say a word slowly. First I'll say (pause) **mmm.** Then I'll say (pause) **at.** Listen again. First I'll say (pause) **mmm.** Then I'll say (pause) **at.**

• Here I go. (Hold up one finger.) **mmm.** (Hold up second finger.) **(mmm)at.**

b. Do it with me. (Hold up one finger.) First you'll say (pause) **mmm.** (Hold up second finger.) Then you'll say (pause) **at.** Get ready. (Say *mmmat* with the children as you hold up a finger for each part.)

c. Again. (Hold up one finger.) First you'll say (pause) **mmm.** (Hold up second finger.) Then you'll say (pause) **at.** Get ready. (Say *mmmat* with the children as you hold up a finger for each part.)

d. (Repeat *c* until firm.)

e. All by yourself. (Hold up one finger.) First you'll say (pause) **mmm.** (Hold up second finger.) Then you'll say (pause) **at.** Get ready. (Hold up one finger, then second finger as the children say *mmmat.*)

f. Again. (Repeat *e* until firm.)

After three words have been presented, following the procedure specified in the format, a less structured presentation is introduced. Notice that the children first indicate both "parts" they are to combine, and then they combine them. This process is very important because it demonstrates how isolated parts are combined to form "words."

Say It Fast—Rhyming Signal

For this exercise, hold up one finger for the first sound and a second finger for the word ending.

Say It Fast—Rhyming Teaching Techniques

- Establish a good rhythm in step *a* and use the same rhythm in steps *b* and *c.* Make sure that the children are responding with you in steps *b* and *c.* They should not lag behind.
- Make sure that you thoroughly firm exercise 10. Children must be able to perform on this exercise perfectly if they are to perform well on later activities.

Beginning at lesson 21, the children are introduced to a variation of the verbal activity that is similar to exercise 10. The children identify the beginning sound, identify the ending, combine the sounds to create a word pronounced slowly, and then say it fast.

Lesson 26 introduces the first rhyming exercise that involves written symbols. The children combine the letter in the Presentation Book with the ending the teacher stipulates. The children say the word slowly, and then say it fast. Notice that the first word is "led" by the teacher. The children are not led on the second word.

Rhyming Signals

When presenting Rhyming formats, you use two signals that you have already practiced. You touch the first ball on an arrow and move under the sound, as you do in the Sounds track. And you slash to signal say it fast as you do in the Sounds—Say It Fast track.

Below is the first Rhyming format, introduced in lesson 26.

Lesson 26

EXERCISE 8

Children identify sounds, then rhyme

a. (Touch the first ball of the arrow for **m.**) My turn. (Move quickly to the second ball.) First I'll say this sound. Then I'll say (pause) ē.
- Listen again. First I'll say this sound. Then I'll say (pause) ē.

b. (Return to the first ball of the arrow.) Here I go. (Move quickly to the second ball and say **mmm.** Slash to the end of the arrow and say:) (mmm)ē.

c. (Return to the first ball of the arrow for **m.**) Do it with me. First you'll say this sound. (Quickly move to the second ball.) Then you'll say (pause) ē. (Slash to the end of the arrow.)
- (Return to the first ball.) Get ready. (Move quickly to the second ball.) *mmm.* (Slash to the end of the arrow.) *(mmm)ē.*

d. (Repeat *b* and *c* until firm.)

e. (Return to the first ball.) Say it fast. (Slash.) *Me.* Yes, **me.**
- Good saying it fast.

f. (Touch the first ball of the arrow for **r.**) Here's a different sound. (Move quickly to the second ball.) First you'll say this sound. Then you'll say (pause) **un.**
- Listen again. First you'll say this sound. Then you'll say (pause) **un.**

g. (Return to the first ball of the arrow.) What sound are you going to say first? (Move quickly to the second ball.) *rrr.*
- Then what will you say? (Slash to the end of the arrow.) *un.*

h. (Return to the first ball of the arrow.) Yes, first you'll say this sound. Then you'll say (pause) **un.** Get ready. (Move quickly to the second ball.) *rrr.* (Slash to the end of the arrow.) *(rrr)un.*

i. (Return to the first ball.) Again. Get ready. (Move quickly to the second ball.) *rrr.* (Slash to the end of the arrow.) *(rrr)un.*

j. (Repeat *i* until firm.)

k. (Return to the first ball.) Say it fast. (Slash.) *Run.*
- Yes, **run.** Good saying it fast.

l. (Call on individual children to do *i* and *k.*)

Other Rhyming Formats

Later formats provide children with practice in rhyming with all the endings they will encounter in beginning reading (**ēēd, an, at, im,** and so forth). The final format in the rhyming sequence (in lesson 36) shows children how to "blend" words that begin with stop sounds.

EXERCISE 3

Children rhyme with **im**

a. (Touch the first ball of the arrow for **r.** Move quickly to the second ball.) You're going to start with this sound and rhyme with (pause) **im.**

b. (Return to the first ball of the arrow.) Tell me the sound you're going to say first. (Move quickly to the second ball.) *rrr.*

• Then what will you say? (Slash to the end of the arrow.) *im.*

c. (Return to the first ball of the arrow.) Again. Tell me the sound you're going to say first. (Move quickly to the second ball.) *rrr.*

• Then what will you say? (Slash to the end of the arrow.) *im.*

d. (Repeat *c* until firm.)

e. (Return to the first ball of the arrow.) Get ready. (Move to the second ball.) *rrr.* (Then slash to the end of the arrow.) *(rrr)im.*

f. (Return to the first ball of the arrow.) Again. Get ready. (Move quickly to the second ball.) *rrr.* (Then slash to the end of the arrow.) *(rrr)im.*

g. (Return to the first ball.) Say it fast. (Slash.) *Rim.*

• Yes, **rim.** You rhymed with (pause) **im.**

h. (Call on individual children to do *f* and *g*.)

i. (Touch the ball of the arrow for **d.**) You're going to start with this sound and rhyme with (pause) **im.**

j. First you'll say this sound. (Slash to the > under **d.**) Then you'll say (pause) **im.** (Slash to the end of the arrow.)

k. (Return to the ball of the arrow.) Tell me the sound you're going to say first. (Slash to the > under **d.**) *d.*

• Then what will you say? (Slash to the end of the arrow.) *im.*

l. (Return to the ball of the arrow.) Again. Tell me the sound you're going to say first. (Slash to the > under **d.**) *d.*

• Then what will you say? (Slash to the end of the arrow.) *im.*

m. (Repeat *l* until firm.)

n. (Return to the ball of the arrow.) Get ready. (Slash to the end of the arrow.) *dim.*

o. (Return to the ball of the arrow.) Again. Get ready. (Slash to the end of the arrow.) *dim.*

p. (Return to the ball of the arrow.) Say it fast. (Slash.) *Dim.*

• Yes, **dim.** You rhymed with (pause) **im.**

q. (Call on individual children to do *l* through *p*.)

Combining a stop-sound beginning like *d* with an ending like *im* is difficult because of the slight change that occurs in the pronunciation of the *d* sound when it is followed by the vowel sound *iii.* The format uses the same ending *(im)* for two beginnings—first a continuous-sound beginning, then a stop-sound beginning.

Rhyming Teaching Techniques

Unless this format is paced rapidly, the children won't see the relationship between **rim** and **dim.** Therefore, correct mistakes and return to the beginning of the format. Also, make liberal use of the individual test at the end of the format (step *q*).

SOUND OUT (Lessons 18–33)

The final prereading track is Sound Out. The activities in this track are similar to those in the Say the Sounds track with one difference. In Say the Sounds, the children repeat the sounds that the teacher says, (*aaammm*). In this track, the children must "read" the sounds. In both Say the Sounds (lessons 6–14) and Sound Out, the children say sounds and do <u>not</u> say it fast.

The sounding-out skill is very important for initial word reading. And the most important part of this skill is saying the sounds of the word *without pausing* or stopping between the sounds. The reason for this is that it is much easier to identify the word if the sounded-out word sounds like the word that is said at a normal speaking rate. The sounded-out word will sound most like the word that is said fast if the sounds are linked together, without pauses between them.

Because appropriate sounding out is so important, the first sounding-out format models the procedure.

Sound Out Signal

The illustration below shows you how to move on the arrow.

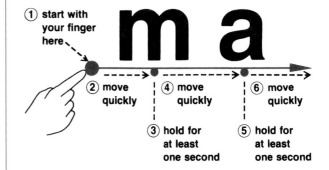

Practice the signal for step *a* without saying your lines. Become firm on the motor behaviors before you present the exercise to your partner. Start on the first ball of the arrow. Move quickly along the arrow, stopping for at least one second at each ball. After you have stopped at the last ball, you may either lift your finger from the page or move quickly to the end of the arrow.

Sound Out Teaching Techniques

- Practice presenting step *a* to your partner. In step *a,* you say **mmmaaa**. Do not pause between the sounds when you move from ball to ball.
- Present step *b* to your partner, who will not make any mistakes. Reinforce the sounding out at step *b* by saying, Good saying **mmmaaa**.
- Practice steps *c* and *d.* Reinforce at step *d* by saying, Good saying **aaammm**.

Lesson 18

EXERCISE 6

Children say the sounds without stopping

a. (Touch the first ball of the arrow for **ma**.) My turn. I'll show you how to say these sounds without stopping between the sounds. (Move under each sound. Hold. Say **mmmaaa**.)

b. (Return to the first ball of the arrow for **ma**.) Your turn. Say the sounds as I touch under them. Don't stop between the sounds. Get ready. (Move under each sound. Hold.) *Mmmaaa.*

- (Return to the first ball of the arrow.) Again. Get ready. (Move under each sound. Hold.) *Mmmaaa.*
- Good saying **mmmaaa**.

c. (Touch the first ball of the arrow for **am**.) My turn. I'll show you how to say these sounds without stopping between the sounds. (Move under each sound. Hold. Say **aaammm**.)

d. (Return to the first ball of the arrow for **am**.) Your turn. Say the sounds as I touch under them. Don't stop between the sounds. Get ready. (Move under each sound. Hold.) *Aaammm.*

- (Return to the first ball of the arrow.) Again. Get ready. (Move under each sound. Hold.) *Aaammm.*
- Good saying **aaammm**.

e. (Call on individual children to do *b* or *d*.)

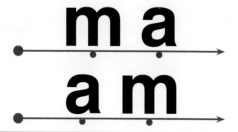

Corrections

If children stop between the sounds at step *b* or *d,* or say the incorrect sounds, stop them immediately. Tell the children what they did, and then repeat step *a* (model) and return to step *b* (test), or repeat *c* and return to *d.*

PREREADING WORKSHEET ACTIVITIES (Lessons 1–39)

The prereading activities you have been practicing are presented through the teacher-presentation material. Other prereading activities are included as part of the daily worksheet activities presented at the end of each lesson. These prereading activities prepare the children for worksheet 34, which is the first worksheet to present word reading exercises.

To prepare for these word-reading exercises, children practice moving their finger under a single sound and saying it, beginning with lesson 1.

Starting in lesson 19, children touch under the sounds of a "word" like **sa**, as they say the sounds.

In worksheet 34, the children touch under the sounds of a word as they say the sounds without stopping between them. Then the children say the word fast.

Worksheet Signal

Because many worksheet exercises require the children to look at symbols on their worksheet, you have to use audible signals to direct them. The simplest signals are taps. The timing for these signals is exactly the same as it is for the other signals you have practiced.

Sound Out Teaching Techniques (.$\frac{s}{\bar{e}}$.)

Part of a worksheet is reproduced below. Note that each sound (**s** and **ē**) is on a ball and arrow. At step *a* children put their finger on the first ball of the first arrow. Children have learned the wording <u>first</u> and <u>next</u> in the Symbol Action Games.

Practice exercise 12 with your partner. Be sure that your partner is touching the correct starting ball. If not, move your partner's finger, and then repeat the step.

Lesson 19

Track 5

EXERCISE 12

Children move their finger under **s** or **ē** and say it

a. Everybody, finger on the first ball of the first arrow. ✔
- When I tap, quickly move your finger under the sound and say it. (Pause.) Get ready. (Tap.) *Children move their finger under* **s** *and say sss.* Yes, **sss.**

b. Again. Finger on the first ball of the first arrow. ✔
- Get ready. (Tap.) *Children move their finger under* **s** *and say sss.* Yes, **sss.**

c. (Repeat *b* until firm.)

d. Everybody, finger on the first ball of the next arrow. ✔
- When I tap, quickly move your finger under the sound and say it. (Pause.) Get ready. (Tap.) *Children move their finger under* **ē** *and say ēēē.* Yes, **ēēē.**

e. Again. Finger on the first ball of the arrow. ✔
- Get ready. (Tap.) *Children move their finger under* **ē** *and say ēēē.* Yes, **ēēē.**

f. (Repeat *e* until firm.)

EXERCISE 13

Individual test

a. (Call on a child. Show the child which ball to touch.) Get ready. (Tap.) *Child moves finger under the sound and says it.*

b. (Call on individual children to do *a.*)

c. Good. You really know how to move your finger under the sound and say it.

Worksheet 19

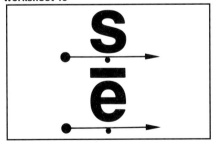

The timing of the tap signal is very important. If the timing is questionable, children will glance up at you. They will be able to respond together and on signal if the time between "Get ready" and the tap is always the same, always predictable. If you

have trouble maintaining a precise time interval, try tapping your foot, as if in time with a march. Time your Get ready . . . (Tap) so that it is in time with the tapping or use a metronome or practice in time with a recording of a march.

Sound Out Teaching Techniques (.$\underline{a\,m}$.)

In the Sound Out exercise on page 30, you moved under the sounds as the children said them. In this format, the children say the sounds and the children move under them.

Lesson 19

EXERCISE 14

Children touch under the sounds

a. (Hold up side 1 of your worksheet. Touch the first ball of the arrow for **am.**) Put your finger on the first ball of this arrow. ✔ (Put down your worksheet.)

b. What's the first sound you'll say? (Signal.) *aaa.*
- What's the next sound you'll say? (Signal.) *mmm.*

c. Everybody, put your finger on the first ball of the arrow. ✔
- When I tap, you're going to quickly move your finger under each sound and say (pause) *aaammm.* Sound it out. Get ready. (Tap for each sound, pausing about two seconds between taps. Check that children are moving their finger under each sound as they say *aaammm.*)

d. Again. Finger on the first ball of the arrow. Get ready. (Tap for each sound, pausing about two seconds between taps. Check that the children are moving their finger under each sound as they say *aaammm.*)

e. (Repeat *d* until firm.)

Worksheet 19

The most important teaching technique is the timing of the exercise. Use the same timing for Get ready . . . *aaammm* as you used for the preceding format (Get ready . . . Tap).

Corrections

If children do not move under the appropriate sound as soon as you tap, guide their finger as you repeat step *c* of the format. After children can perform with no prompting (such as guiding their finger), repeat step *c* at least two or three more times, until the children are quite firm in their response.

If children have trouble when you call on them for individual turns, repeat step *c* with the group.

READING

Lessons 1 to 27 set the stage for word reading. Starting at lesson 28, the children begin to read simple, regular words by sounding out each word and saying it fast. In *Reading Mastery,* Grade K, sounds and words are introduced on a closely integrated schedule:

1. Throughout the program, the children learn sounds at the rate of about one every three to four lessons. Forty sounds are taught.

2. By lesson 28 the children have learned six sounds. The children begin to read words containing those sounds. As each new sound is taught, the sound is introduced in words.

3. After a word has been taught and practiced, the word is incorporated in stories or sentences. Once a word has been introduced, it is used throughout the remainder of the program.

4. The children begin to read very short, single-sentence stories in lesson 48. During the last part of the program, they read stories of over one hundred words every day.

5. The children practice words and sentences in the independent work on their worksheets.

Comprehension activities are specified in word-reading, story-reading, and worksheet activities. Story reading starts with basic, literal-comprehension questions. As the children become more proficient, they work on more elaborate comprehension activities, which require judgments or predictions about story events.

HOW TO USE THE READING SECTION OF THE GUIDE

The Reading section of this guide consists of two primary tracks: Reading Vocabulary and Story Reading. Starting at lesson 40, you present both tracks every day.

After you have introduced all the prereading skills to the children, and before you reach lesson 28, you should begin studying and practicing the reading exercises. You may want to do this in three phases:

Phase I: Before your top group reaches lesson 28
Reading Vocabulary. Read the overview (page 33) and practice the formats for regular words (pages 34–37) and rhyming words (pages 38–39).
Story Reading. Read the overview (pages 44–45) and practice the formats for sound it out and say it fast (pages 46–50).

Phase II: When your top group reaches lesson 50
Reading Vocabulary. Practice the formats for reading the fast way (pages 40–42).
Story Reading. Practice the formats for reading the fast way (pages 51–57).

Phase III: When your top group reaches lesson 80
Reading Vocabulary. Practice the formats for irregular words (page 43) and read the information on other reading vocabulary formats (page 44).
Story Reading. Review the materials on individual Fluency Checkouts (pages 57–58) and additional reading (page 59), and practice the format for Read the Items (pages 58–59).

READING VOCABULARY
Lessons (28–160)

OVERVIEW

1. The first word-reading (reading vocabulary) formats are introduced in lesson 28. In lessons 34 to 39, the children read words on their worksheets. Beginning at lesson 40, the children read stories composed of words that have been introduced earlier.

2. The first reading-vocabulary words begin with continuous sounds like **a, m, s,** or **th.** Some words may end with a stop sound like **d, t,** or **c,** but none begin with stop sounds. The reason is that sounding out a word that begins with a stop sound is much more difficult than sounding out a word that begins with a continuous sound. Words beginning with stop sounds are introduced at lesson 43, after the children have been reading simple, regular words for fifteen lessons.

3. In lesson 42, the first "slightly irregular" word is taught. The word is **is.** It is irregular because it is sounded out as **iiiss** (which rhymes with **miss**) but is pronounced **iz.** You direct the children to sound out the word **is,** and then "translate" by saying, Yes, **iz.** We say **iz.** She **is** happy.

   Other slightly irregular words presented in early lessons are **a** and **has.** The purpose of introducing words that are slightly irregular is to make the children aware that not everything they read is perfectly regular. By introducing some words that are not perfectly regular early in the reading program, you alert the children to what will come. Note that children still sound out all words—regular or irregular—but they learn to discriminate between how the irregular word is sounded out and how it is pronounced.

4. Highly irregular words are introduced after children have mastered slightly irregular words. The procedure is the same—children always say the sound they have learned for each letter. In sounding out a word such as **was,** they say **wwwaaasss** (rhymes with mass.) Then you translate, That's how we <u>**sound out**</u> the word. Here's how we say the word. Wuz. After several lessons, the children read the whole word the fast way and <u>then</u> sound it out. The sounding-out decoding skill eliminates guessing. Irregulars are not treated as "sight" words because a particular word, like was, is always spelled the same way. The sounding out demonstrates this stable spelling.

5. Children begin to read words the fast way in lesson 60. By lesson 96 children read all words the fast way.

A variety of word-attack skills is taught. The same word may appear in a rhyming format, a sound-out format, a read-the-fast-way format, and a build-up format.

The reading-vocabulary portion of the lesson should take no more than ten minutes early in the program and less later in the program, so that an increasing amount of the lesson time can be spent on the stories. The exercises in this guide will help you teach economically.

Although the emphasis of the reading-vocabulary activities is on decoding, we want to make sure the children understand that they are reading real words. Therefore, the program specifies "meaning" sentences to be presented after children read certain words. For instance, after they read the word **meat** in lesson 46, you are instructed to say, A hamburger is made of (pause) **meat.** Meaning sentences are not specified for all words. If you feel that a sentence would help the children understand a particular word that may not be well understood in isolation, put it in a sentence. But <u>don't</u> use the meaning sentence as a substitute for decoding. Children do not become facile at decoding words by understanding the words. They become facile at decoding by practicing decoding.

Regular words, such as in the sentence **Pam had a ham,** are easy to read. Each word can be sounded out and said fast without mispronouncing the word. But the number of simple, regular words is very limited. To increase the number of "regular" words (words that children can pronounce the way they are sounded out), *Reading Mastery*, Grade K uses a modified orthography, or print, which is faded out in Grade 1 of the *Reading Mastery* program.

The modified orthography presents three conventions:

1. *Diacritical marks.* Long lines appear over the symbols for the vowels that sound like their letter names (ā, ē, ī, ō, ū). The symbol **a** signals the sound in **at**, while **ā** signals the sound in **ate**.

2. *Small letters.* Small letters appear in some words. Children are taught to sound out only full-size letters, not small ones. The small letters permit many words with silent letters to be spelled correctly. As the children progress through the program, the small letters are increased in size. The examples below illustrate the long lines and small letters:

māil   kick   ēat   have
hōme

3. *Joined letters.* If two or more letters function as a single sound, they are joined. The joined letters allow many additional words to become regular words.

shop   that   her
tēacher   slīding

Children Say the Sounds, Then Sound Out the Word (Lessons 28–34)

The first reading-vocabulary format requires a simple extension of the behaviors that have been taught in the say it fast—rhyming, the rhyming, and the sound-out formats. Note that the children read words that are presented on an arrow, with a ball beneath each sound. After lesson 53, the arrow is retained, but the balls are removed.

Lesson 28

Track 8

EXERCISE 6
Children say the sounds, then sound out the word

a. (Point to the first ball of the arrow for **am.**) This is the word (pause) **am.** What word? (Touch the first ball.) *Am.* Yes, **am.**

b. (Point to the ball for **a.**) When you sound out (pause) **am,** what sound do you say first? (Touch the ball for **a.**) *aaa.* Yes, **aaa.**

• (Point to the ball for **m.**) What sound do you say next? (Touch the ball for **m.**) *mmm.* Yes, **mmm.**

c. (Repeat *b* until firm.)

d. (Return to the first ball.) You're going to sound it out, then say it fast. Everybody, sound it out. Get ready. (Move under each sound. Hold under each sound for two seconds.) *Aaammm.*

e. (Return to the first ball.) Again. Sound it out. Get ready. (Move under each sound. Hold under each sound for two seconds.) *Aaammm.*

f. (Repeat *e* until firm.)

g. (Return to the first ball.) Say it fast. (Slash to the end of the arrow.) *Am.* Yes, **am.**

• You read the word (pause) **am.** I (pause) **am** (pause) happy.

h. (Call on individual children to do *e* and *g*.)

Point and Touch Signal
The signal in steps *a* through *c* is different from those you practiced earlier. In step *a*, you point to the starting ball for the word without touching the ball. Then you touch it. Your touch is the signal for the children to respond.

In steps *b* and *c*, you point to the ball for a sound. Then you touch the ball. The children respond when you touch. Be sure you lift your finger when you move along the arrow so you can point to the next sound without touching it.

Practice pointing and touching in steps *a* through *c*. When you point, be careful not to hold your finger so you hide part of the sound from the children's view. Point from below, and use the same timing that you use for all other signals.

Sound It Out—Say It Fast Signal

The signal you will use to direct the children to sound out words in steps *d* through *g* of this format (and in all sound-out formats until lesson 160) is exactly the same as you practiced in Sound Out (page 30). After the children sound out the word, you direct them to say it fast.

The illustration below demonstrates the correct procedures for presenting the word **meat** from lesson 46. Practice this procedure.

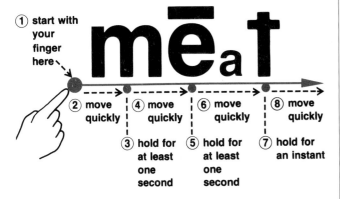

① start with your finger here

② move quickly
③ hold for at least one second
④ move quickly
⑤ hold for at least one second
⑥ move quickly
⑦ hold for an instant
⑧ move quickly

⑨ return to the first ball

⑩ quickly move along arrow for say-it-fast signal

- Hold under the **m** for at least one second; hold under the **ē** for at least one second; move past the **a** (it has no ball under it); hold under the **t** for only an instant; and then move quickly to the end of the arrow. The children respond, *mmmēēēt*.

- After you reach the end of the arrow, return to the first ball of the arrow. Say, Say it fast. Pause one second. Then slash from the first ball to the end of the arrow. The children respond, *meat*. Remember, first you talk—then you signal. Practice this timing. Start with your finger on the first ball. Keep your finger on the ball as you say, Say it fast . . . and pause one second. Signal by slashing along the arrow.

Practice exercise 6 from the beginning, with your partner making no mistakes.

Corrections

Lesson 28

EXERCISE 6

Children say the sounds, then sound out the word

a. (Point to the first ball of the arrow for **am**.) This is the word (pause) **am**. What word? (Touch the first ball.) *Am*. Yes, **am**.

b. (Point to the ball for **a**.) When you sound out (pause) **am**, what sound do you say first? (Touch the ball for **a**.) *aaa*. Yes, **aaa**.

• (Point to the ball for **m**.) What sound do you say next? (Touch the ball for **m**.) *mmm*. Yes, **mmm**.

c. (Repeat *b* until firm.)

d. (Return to the first ball.) You're going to sound it out, then say it fast. Everybody, sound it out. Get ready. (Move under each sound. Hold under each sound for two seconds.) *Aaammm*.

e. (Return to the first ball.) Again. Sound it out. Get ready. (Move under each sound. Hold under each sound for two seconds.) *Aaammm*.

f. (Repeat *e* until firm.)

g. (Return to the first ball.) Say it fast. (Slash to the end of the arrow.) *Am*. Yes, **am**.

• You read the word (pause) **am**. I (pause) **am** (pause) happy.

h. (Call on individual children to do *e* and *g*.)

1. If the children don't respond firmly for each sound, say, Starting over . . . and repeat step *b* until the children reliably say both sounds. Present a delayed test by repeating steps *a* through *c*.

2. Use the correction below for steps *d* through *h* if a child breaks between the sounds (*aaa . . . mmm*) or is unable to say the word fast after sounding it out (*aaammm*). Your correction will show the children how word reading relates to the oral blending exercises they have already learned.

1. Teacher: Everybody, say (pause) **aaammm**. Get ready. (Hold up a finger for each sound.)
2. Group: *aaammm*.
3. Teacher: Say it fast. (Drop your hand.)
4. Group: *am*.
5. Teacher: (Quickly touch the first ball for **am**.) Now do it here. Sound it out. Get ready. (Move quickly under each sound. Hold under each sound for two seconds.)
6. Group: *aaammm*.
7. Teacher: (Return to the first ball.) Say it fast. (Slash to the end of the arrow.)
8. Group: *am*.
9. Teacher: You did it.

If the mistake occurred on an individual turn, after correcting the group with steps 1 to 8, present steps e and g to the child who made the mistake.

Children Think about the Sounds, Then Sound Out the Word
(Lessons 35–41)

During this lesson range, increasing demands are placed on the children through a series of small changes in the directions they are given. The first change involves identifying individual sounds before sounding out a word. In earlier formats, you directed the identification of each sound before directing the children to sound out the word. At lesson 40, you simply direct the children to think about the sounds, without saying them out loud.

Lesson 40

EXERCISE 5

Children think about the sounds, then sound out the word

a. (Touch the first ball of the arrow for **this**.) I'll move down the arrow and stop under the sounds. But don't say the sounds out loud. Just figure out what you're going to say. (Move quickly under each sound.) *Children do not respond.*

b. (Return to the first ball. Pause for three seconds.) Sound it out. Get ready. (Move quickly under each sound.) *Thththiiisss.*

c. (Return to the first ball.) Again, sound it out. Get ready. (Move quickly under each sound.) *Thththiiisss.*

d. (Repeat *c* until firm.)

e. (Return to the first ball.) Say it fast. (Slash.) *This.*

• Yes, what word? (Signal.) *This.*

• I like (pause) **this** (pause) book.

f. (Call on individual children to do *c* and *e*.)

• *Step a.* Watch the children's eyes as they sound out the word to themselves. Tell them to sound out silently or whisper. Come on. Figure out what you're going to say. If the children produce no mouth movements, or if they have trouble in step *b,* tell them, Whisper the sounds to yourselves. Just don't say them out loud. Repeat step *a.*

• *Step b.* Remember to pause for three seconds before telling the children to sound it out. This thinking time is very important. To help you pace the three-second pause, tap your foot three beats.

Children Sound Out the Word and Say It Fast (Lessons 40–55)

During these lessons, the children read a group of words on a page. A performance criterion is specified. The group must read all the words on the page in order without making a mistake before you present the next page. The children will make some mistakes. When they make a mistake on a word, you correct the mistake and go to the next word. When you finish the last word, you tell the children, That was pretty good. Let's read the words again. See if you can read them without making a mistake.

Return to the first word on the page and present all the words in order until the children meet the page criterion.

Note: The word **is** is slightly irregular. It is sounded out as **iiisss,** but it is pronounced **iz,** not **iss.** When this word was first introduced in lesson 42, the children sounded it out and said it fast, **iss,** after which you said, Yes, **iz.** We say **iz.** She (pause) **is** happy. By lesson 46, the children continue to sound out the word as *iiisss,* but they are familiar enough with the word to pronounce it correctly when you tell them to say it fast.

READING VOCABULARY

Do not touch any small letters.

As soon as you read all the words on this page without making a mistake, we'll go on to the next page.

EXERCISE 6

Children sound out the word and say it fast

a. (Touch the first ball of the arrow for **sad.**) Sound it out. Get ready. (Move quickly under each sound.) *Sssaaad.*
b. (Return to the first ball.) Again, sound it out. Get ready. (Move quickly under each sound.) *Sssaaad.*
c. (Repeat *b* until firm.)
d. (Return to the first ball.) Say it fast. (Slash.) *Sad.*
• Yes, what word? (Signal.) *Sad.*

EXERCISE 7

Children sound out the word and say it fast

a. (Touch the first ball of the arrow for **ēat.**) Sound it out. Get ready. (Move quickly under each sound.) *Ēēēt.*
b. (Return to the first ball.) Again, sound it out. Get ready. (Move quickly under each sound.) *Ēēēt.*
c. (Repeat *b* until firm.)
d. (Return to the first ball.) Say it fast. (Slash.) *Eat.*
• Yes, what word? (Signal.) *Eat.* She likes to (pause) **eat.**

EXERCISE 8

Children sound out the word and say it fast

a. (Touch the first ball of the arrow for **sat.**) Sound it out. Get ready. (Move quickly under each sound.) *Sssaaat.*
b. (Return to the first ball.) Again, sound it out. Get ready. (Move quickly under each sound.) *Sssaaat.*
c. (Repeat *b* until firm.)
d. (Return to the first ball.) Say it fast. (Slash.) *Sat.*
• Yes, what word? (Signal.) *Sat.*

EXERCISE 9

Children sound out the word and say it fast

a. (Touch the first ball of the arrow for **mēat.**) Sound it out. Get ready. (Move quickly under each sound.) *Mmmēēēt.*
b. (Return to the first ball.) Again, sound it out. Get ready. (Move quickly under each sound.) *Mmmēēēt.*
c. (Repeat *b* until firm.)
d. (Return to the first ball.) Say it fast. (Slash.) *Meat.*
• Yes, what word? (Signal.) *Meat.*
• A hamburger is made of (pause) **meat.**

EXERCISE 10

Children sound out the word and say it fast

a. (Touch the first ball of the arrow for **is.**) Sound it out. Get ready. (Move quickly under each sound.) *iiisss.* (Children should not say **iiizzz.**)
b. (Return to the first ball.) Again, sound it out. Get ready. (Move quickly under each sound.) *iiisss.*
c. (Repeat *b* until firm.)
d. (Return to the first ball.) Say it fast. (Slash.) *Is.*
• Yes, **iz.** We say **iz.**
• **Is** (pause) it raining today?

CRITERION

(If the children read the words in exercises 6, 7, 8, 9, and 10 without making any mistakes, present individual turns.)
(If the children made mistakes, say:) That was pretty good. Let's read the words again. See if you can read them without making a mistake.

EXERCISE 11

Individual test

(Call on individual children. Each child is to do exercise 6, 7, 8, 9, or 10.)

Beginning at lesson 37, the children read some words as rhyming words by applying the rhyming skills practiced in the oral-rhyming tracks.

The rhyming skill allows the children to read many new words by blending different initial sounds with word endings. A child with good rhyming skills can see that words that rhyme have ending parts that sound alike and look alike.

In rhyming formats from lessons 37 to 56, two or more words in a series are presented. The rhyming part of each word is in red type. The beginning sounds are in black type. Children sound out and then identify the ending part. Then they identify the beginning sound and blend it with the ending part. Their behavior is very similar to that called for in the oral-rhyming formats.

Rhyming—Words That Begin with Continuous Sounds

- *Steps b to d.* Use the same signal as you practiced in the sound it out—say it fast formats on page 35.
- *Step e.* Keep your finger on the first ball of the arrow for **sēēd** as you ask, So what does this word rhyme with? (Tap the ball.) The children respond *ēēd.* (Keep touching the first ball until after you say:) Rhyme with (pause) **ēēd.** Get ready . . . (Move quickly to the second ball and hold.) The children respond *sss.* When you slash, they complete the unblended word—*sssēēd.* (Return to the first ball. Keep touching the ball as you ask:) What word? (Pause one second. Slash.) The children should say, *sēēd.*

Corrections—Step e

1. When you tap the first ball of the arrow, the children may respond by saying *sss* because they are not attending to your question. If they say *sss,* correct by saying, **ēēd.** It rhymes with **ēēd.** Listen again. Repeat step e from the beginning.

2. When you hold your finger under the **s,** the children are supposed to hold the **sss** until you slash. If a child says *sssēēd* before you slash, tell the group, I'm still touching under the **sss.** Repeat step e from Rhyme with (pause) **ēēd.** Get ready, until the children are firm at holding the **sss.**

Lesson 40   Track 9

EXERCISE 8

Children rhyme with **ēēd**

a. (Point to **ēēd, sēēd,** and **fēēd.**) These words rhyme.

b. (Touch the first ball of the arrow for **ēēd.** Pause.) Sound it out. Get ready. (Move quickly under each sound.) *ēēēd.*

c. (Return to the first ball.) Again, sound it out. Get ready. (Move quickly under each sound.) *Ēēēd.*

d. (Return to the first ball.) Say it fast. (Slash.) *Ēēd.* Yes, **ēēd.**

e. (Touch the first ball of the arrow for **sēēd.**) The red part of this word is (pause) **ēēd.** So what does this word rhyme with? (Tap the ball.) *Ēēd.* Yes, **ēēd.**
- Rhyme with (pause) **ēēd.** Get ready. (Move quickly to the second ball. Hold.) *sss.* (Slash.) *Sssēēd.*
- (Return to the first ball.) What word? (Slash.) *Seed.* Yes, **seed.**

f. (Touch the first ball of the arrow for **fēēd.**) The red part of this word is (pause) **ēēd.** So what does this word rhyme with? (Tap the ball.) *Ēēd.* Yes, **ēēd.**
- Rhyme with (pause) **ēēd.** Get ready. (Move quickly to the second ball. Hold.) *fff.* (Slash.) *Fffēēd.*
- (Return to the first ball.) What word? (Slash.) *Feed.* Yes, **feed.**

g. (Call on individual children to do e or f.)

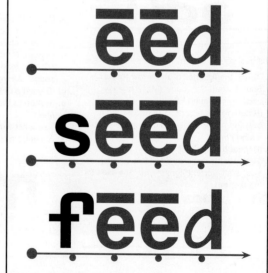

Rhyming—Words That Begin with Stop Sounds

Words that begin with stop sounds, such as **c, d,** or **t,** are hard for children to sound out because the sound cannot be held for more than an instant. If the sound is held longer, it becomes distorted with an inappropriate vowel sound—**duuuuuu.** A variation of the word-rhyming format teaches children to process words that begin with stop sounds (lessons 43 to 56).

Lesson 48

EXERCISE 15

Children rhyme with **an**

  a. (Point to **an** and **dan.**) These words rhyme.
  b. (Touch the first ball of the arrow for **an.** Pause.) Sound it out. Get ready. (Move quickly under each sound.) *Aaannn.*
  c. (Return to the first ball.) Again, sound it out. Get ready. (Move quickly under each sound.) *Aaannn.*
  d. (Return to the first ball.) Say it fast. (Slash.) *An.* Yes, **an.**
  e. (Touch the first ball of the arrow for **dan.**) This word rhymes with (pause) **an.** Say it fast and rhyme with (pause) **an.** (Pause.) Get ready. (Slash.) *Dan.* Yes, **dan.**
  f. (Return to the first ball for **dan.**) Again, rhyme with (pause) **an.** Get ready. (Slash.) *Dan.* Yes, **dan.**
  g. (Repeat f until firm.)
  h. (Call on individual children to do f.)

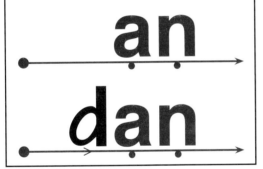

The arrowhead prompts children to say the sound fast and to blend the sound with the ending part of the word. If the stop sound appears at the end of a word, it has a ball under it rather than an arrowhead because the children stop at the end of a word.

Children Read a Word Beginning with a Stop Sound

This format, which starts at lesson 63, contains fewer prompts than earlier rhyming formats. The children first identify the ending part of the word (for example, **it**), and then they rhyme. Note that there are no balls or arrowheads on the arrow shaft.

Lesson 63

EXERCISE 17

Children read a word beginning with a stop sound (**hit**)

  a. (Run your finger under **it.**) You're going to sound out this part. Get ready. (Touch **i, t** as the children say *iiit.*)
  b. Say it fast. (Signal.) *It.* Yes, this part says (pause) **it.**
  c. (Repeat a and b until firm.)
  d. (Touch the ball for **hit.**) This word rhymes with (pause) **it.** Get ready. (Move quickly along the arrow.) *Hit.*
  e. What word? (Signal.) *Hit.* Yes, **hit.**
  f. (Repeat d and e until firm.)
  g. (Return to the ball.) Now you're going to sound out (pause) **hit.** Get ready. (Quickly touch **h, i, t** as the children say *hiiit.*)
  h. What word? (Signal.) *Hit.* Yes, **hit.**
  • Good reading. She **hit** me.
  i. (Repeat g and h until firm.)

• *Step a.* Run your finger under **it** to identify the part of the word the children are to sound out. Do not permit them to start sounding out with **h.** If necessary, cover the **h.**

• *Step b.* You say, "Say it fast," and not "What word?" because the ending part of a stop-sound word is not always a word by itself (<u>t</u>ail, <u>c</u>op, <u>h</u>e).

• *Step d.* Quickly touch **h** for only an instant, and then slash under the rest of the word as the children say *hit.*

• *Step g.* Touch the **h** for only an instant, and then move to **i.** The illustration below shows your behavior for directing the sounding out of his word, which begins (and ends) with a stop sound.

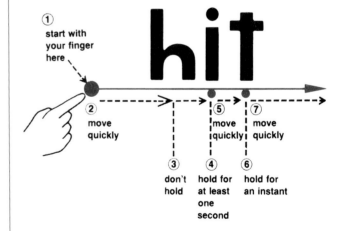

Correction

If children have trouble with step *g,* remind them, You have to say this first sound fast. So I can't stop under it. When I stop under the next sound, say both sounds.

The sequence of formats in this track is designed to help the children make the transition from sounding out every word to reading new words without sounding them out. Beginning at lesson 60, the children read a word the fast way after they have sounded out the word and identified it.

Lesson 60

EXERCISE 8
Children sound out the word, then read it the fast way

a. (Touch the ball for **thē**.) Sound it out.
b. Get ready. (Touch **th**, **ē** as the children say *thththēēē*.)
• (If sounding out is not firm, repeat *b*.)
c. What word? (Signal.) *Thē*. Yes, **thē**.
d. (Return to the ball.) Get ready to read the word the fast way. Don't sound it out. Just tell me the word.
e. (Pause at least three seconds.) Get ready. (Move your finger quickly along the arrow.) *Thē*.
• Yes, **thē**. Good reading.

┌─**To Correct**─────────────────────────
│ If the children sound out the word instead of reading it the fast way
│ 1. (Say:) I'll read the word the <u>fast</u> way. **Thē**.
│ 2. (Repeat *d* and *e* until firm.)
│ 3. (Repeat *a* through *e*.)
└───────────────────────────────

f. (Repeat *d* and *e* until firm.)

• *Step b.* Touch under each sound as the children sound out the word. Slash under the word as the children respond to What word?

• *Step e.* Pause at least three seconds. The idea is to build the child's "memory" for handling words. If you proceed too fast from *c* through *e,* very little memory load will be placed on the child. In later formats, the memory load will be further increased until the children are able to remember words consistently from one day to the next.

• *Steps d and e.* Expect to repeat these steps at least one time the first time this format is presented.

Correction

If a child misidentifies the word at step *e,* correct by returning to step *a* and repeating the exercise.

Track Development

In the format for **thē** below, you count to five before directing the children to identify the word. The purpose of the counting is to challenge the children to remember the word in the face of greater "interference."

Lesson 65

EXERCISE 6
Children sound out the word, then read it the fast way

a. (Touch the ball for **thē**.) Sound it out.
b. Get ready. (Touch **th**, **ē** as the children say *thththēēē*.)
• (If sounding out is not firm, repeat *b*.)
c. What word? (Signal.) *Thē*. Yes, **thē**.
d. (Return to the ball.) Get ready to read the word the fast way. I'm going to count to five. See if you can remember the word.
e. 1, 2, 3, 4, 5. Get ready. (Move your finger quickly along the arrow.) *Thē*. Yes, **thē**.
• Good reading.
f. Again. (Repeat *e* until firm.)

Some words are in shaded boxes. The children have read these words earlier in the lesson.

Lesson 65

EXERCISE 17
Children read the word in the box the fast way

a. (Touch the ball for **not**.)
b. You're going to read this word the fast way. I'll move down the arrow and stop under the sounds. But don't say the sounds out loud. Just figure out what you're going to say. (Touch under each sound.) *Children do not respond.*
c. (Return to the ball. Pause at least three seconds.) Read it the fast way. Get ready. (Slash.) *Not*. Yes, **not**.

Word identification mistakes are corrected by first directing the children to sound out the word and then repeating the exercise.

A reading-vocabulary page from lesson 75 is reproduced below. Exercises 15 and 16 are rhyming exercises.

Lesson 75

EXERCISE 15

Children rhyme with **sick**

a. (Touch the ball for **sick.**) Sound it out.

b. Get ready. (Touch **s, i, c** as the children say *sssiiic.*)
- (If sounding out is not firm, repeat *b.*)

c. What word? (Signal.) *Sick.* Yes, **sick.**

d. (Quickly touch the ball for **lick.**) This word rhymes with (pause) **sick.** Get ready. (Touch **l.**) *lll.*
- (Move quickly along the arrow.) *Lllick.*

e. What word? (Signal.) *Lick.* Yes, **lick.**

EXERCISE 16

Children read a word beginning with a stop sound (**hāte**)

a. (Run your finger under **ate.**) You're going to sound out this part. Get ready. (Touch **ā, t** as the children say *aaat.*)

b. Say it fast. (Signal.) *Ate.*
- Yes, this part says (pause) **ate.**

c. (Repeat *a* and *b* until firm.)

d. (Touch the ball for **hāte.**) This word rhymes with (pause) **āāt.** Get ready. (Move quickly along the arrow.) *Hate.*

e. What word? (Signal.) *Hate.* Yes, **hate.**

f. (Repeat *d* and *e* until firm.)

g. (Return to the ball.) Now you're going to sound out (pause) **hate.** Get ready. (Quickly touch **h, ā, t** as the children say *hāāāt.*)

h. What word? (Signal.) *Hate.* Yes, **hate.**
- Good reading. Do you **hate** monsters?

i. (Repeat *g* and *h* until firm.)

EXERCISE 17

Children read a word beginning with a stop sound (**cāme**)

(Repeat the procedures in exercise 16 for **cāme.**)

EXERCISE 18

Children read the words the fast way

a. Now you get to read these words the fast way.

b. (Touch the ball for **lick.** Pause three seconds.) Get ready. (Move your finger quickly along the arrow.) *Lick.*

c. (Repeat *b* for **sick, hāte,** and **cāme.**)

d. (Have the children sound out the words they had difficulty identifying.)

EXERCISE 19

Individual test

(Call on individual children to read one word the fast way.)

Children Read the Words the Fast Way

Children reread the words the fast way on some reading-vocabulary pages in lessons 75 to 160. Sometimes the words have been sounded out; sometimes they have been presented in a rhyme series; or sometimes they have been read the fast way. The rereading step is designed to help children with whole-word reading and with remembering words.

Correcting Word-Identification Mistakes in Lists of Words

In lessons 56 to 160, the children read words in columns. If a child misidentifies one of the words in a column, use the correction procedure below. Use the same procedure whether the word was presented in a sound-out format, a rhyming format, or in a read-the-fast-way format. As in all corrections, correct the group.

Here are the steps in the correction procedure:

1. Identify the word. That word is . . .
2. Direct the group to sound out and identify the word. Everybody, sound it out . . . Get ready . . . What word?
3. Direct the group to return to the first word in the column. Starting over . . . or Back to the first word in the column . . .
4. Return to the ball for the first word on the page; pause several seconds; then ask What word? for each word on the page.

If the mistake occurs on an individual test in which a child is reading only one word, correct with steps 1 to 4 above. Present additional individual turns. Then return to the child who missed the word and have that child sound out and identify the word.

Children Read the Fast Way

Beginning at lesson 96, the children read all the words on the page the fast way and then read the words in a new, random order as specified in the format. Beginning at lesson 96, most words will be taught in this format.

Lesson 96

> **To Correct**
> (For all mistakes, have the children sound out the word and say it fast. Then say:) Remember this word.

EXERCISE 13

Children read the fast way

a. Get ready to read these words the fast way.
b. (Touch the ball for **this.** Pause three seconds.) Get ready. (Signal.) *This.*
c. (Touch the ball for **that.** Pause three seconds.) Get ready. (Signal.) *That.*
d. (Repeat c for **thē.**)

EXERCISE 14

Children read the fast way again

a. Get ready to do these words again. Watch where I point.
b. (Point to a word. Pause one second. Say:) Get ready. (Signal.) *The children respond.*
• (Point to the words in this order: **thē, that, this.**)
c. (Repeat b until firm.)

EXERCISE 15

Individual test

(Call on individual children to read one word in exercise 14 the fast way.)

this

that

thē

• Treat the page as a unit. The children must be able to read all the words on the page correctly before moving to the next page.

• Follow the specified variation in order when the children reread the words. Varying the original order will show you just how firm the children really are on all the words.

• In the rereading, pause one second after pointing to a word before signaling for the children to say the word. If you signal without pausing, they will probably have difficulty responding correctly.

IRREGULAR WORDS
(Lessons 89–160)

Before lesson 89 you introduced slightly irregular words, such as **has, is, a.** Now you will introduce somewhat more irregular words, such as **was, of, said, boy.** In *Reading Mastery,* Grade K, a word is irregular if it is sounded out one way and pronounced (said fast) another.

An irregular word is introduced in stages through several lessons. In the first stage, the word is sounded out and then pronounced as it is usually said. In the next stage, the word is identified by reading it the fast way, and then sounding it out. The word then appears on reading-vocabulary pages to be read the fast way.

Children Sound Out an Irregular Word (First Format)

Lesson 89   Track 11

EXERCISE 8

Children sound out an irregular word (said)

a. (Touch the ball for **said.**) Sound it out.
b. Get ready. (Quickly touch each sound as the children say *sssaaaiiid.*)

To Correct
If the children sound out the word as **sssĕĕĕd**
1. (Say:) You've got to say the sounds I touch.
2. (Repeat *a* and *b* until firm.)

c. Again. (Repeat *b* until firm.)
d. That's how we <u>sound out</u> the word. Here's how we <u>say</u> the word. **Said.** How do we <u>say</u> the word? (Signal.) *Said.*
e. Now you're going to <u>sound out</u> the word. Get ready. (Touch each sound as the children say *sssaaaiiid.*)
f. Now you're going to <u>say</u> the word. Get ready. (Signal.) *Said.*
g. (Repeat *e* and *f* until firm.)
h. Yes, this word is **said.** She **said,** "Hello."

said

- *Step d.* Emphasize the words "sound out" and "say." Pause slightly to set off the words. That's how we (pause) **<u>sound out</u>** the word. Here's how we (pause) **<u>say</u>** the word. **Said.** How do we (pause) **<u>say</u>** the word? (Signal by slashing along the arrow.)
- *Steps e and f.* Repeat these steps in sequence at least two times. With very low-performing children, you may have to present the sequence four or five times before the children are firm. Expect these children to have difficulty with the first two or three irregular words that are introduced.

Corrections

1. In step *e,* if the children sound out the word the way it is pronounced, use the correction in the format.

2. In step *f,* if the children begin to sound out the word when told to say the word or if they say the wrong word, correct as follows:

step f ⟶ Now you're going to say the word. Get ready. (Signal.)
mistake ⟶ Children say *sssaaaiiid* or *was.* Correct by saying, That word is **said.** Say the word. Get ready. (Signal.) *Said (sed).* Now sound out the word. Get ready. (Signal.) *Sssaaaiiid.* Let's try it again. Return to step *a.*

Children Sound Out an Irregular Word (Second Format)

After three lessons the irregular word is taught with this format.

Lesson 92

EXERCISE 7

Children identify, then sound out an irregular word (said)

a. (Touch the ball for **said.**) Everybody, you're going to read this word the fast way. (Pause three seconds.) Get ready. (Move your finger quickly along the arrow.) *Said.* Yes, **said.**
b. Now you're going to sound out the word. Get ready. (Quickly touch **s, a, i, d** as the children say *sssaaaiiid.*)
c. Again. (Repeat *b.*)
d. How do we say the word? (Signal.) *Said.* Yes, **said.**
e. (Repeat *b* and *d* until firm.)

said

- *Step a.* Be sure to pause three seconds to give the children thinking time.

Corrections
Use the same corrections as for the first irregular-word format (lesson 89, exercise 8.)

Special Word-Analysis Formats

Beginning with lesson 96, children read the vocabulary words the fast way, except in the following special word-analysis formats.

Ending Build-Ups (Lessons 124–160)

kiss
kissed

The children read the first word, *kiss.* You touch the ball for **kiss** and say, "Yes, this word is **kiss.**" You quickly touch the ball for **kissed** and say, "So this must be **kiiiiisssssss . . .**" and point to the **d** before touching it. When you touch the **d,** the children say *kissed.* Then they sound out the word. You signal for the sounding-out as you would if the word were on an arrow like the one below.

kissed

Move quickly from the **k** to the **i,** then to between the two **s**'s, and then to the **d.**

In teaching this particular build-up, avoid referring to the ending as "the e-d ending." Such a reference might lead the children to mispronounce the ending. In some of the words the children read, the ending is pronounced **d** as in **rained;** in others it's pronounced **t** as in **kissed.** If children pronounce **kissed** with a **d** sound, say, "Yes, **kisst.** What word?"

Words Beginning with Two Consonants (Lessons 130–160)

slip

You cover the **s;** the children identify the last part of the word—*lip.* You uncover the **s** and tell the children, "First you say **sss;** then you say **lip.**" The children blend *ssslip,* and then say it fast. After they are firm, the children sound out the word.

Story Reading (Lessons 40–160)

The content of the stories is based on two main criteria: First, the words used in the stories are coordinated carefully with the words introduced in the reading-vocabulary presentations. Words are generally presented in the reading-vocabulary presentation for a few days before they are introduced in the stories. Second, the stories and art are designed to be interesting, amusing, and appealing to the children.

All story-reading exercises are part of the structured lesson. They follow the sounds and reading-vocabulary exercises. The allotted lesson time permits the group to read each story more than one time. Initially, the stories are not the major part of the reading lesson. By lesson 75, however, most of the lesson time is spent on story reading.

The stories increase in length from two words in lesson 40 to more than one hundred fifty words by lesson 160. At the end of their first year of reading instruction, children in *Reading Mastery,* Grade K are able to read stories that are more sophisticated than those presented in other reading programs.

OVERVIEW

The major topics in the story track are outlined in the scope and sequence chart on page 76. In this story section of the guide, each topic is described and teaching techniques and corrections are provided.

Sounding Out Words (Lessons 28–74)

During this lesson range, children sound out each word and then say it fast. Sounding out begins in reading vocabulary at lesson 28. The children sound out one word on their worksheets in lessons 34 to 39. From lessons 40 to 47, they sound out two words on their worksheets. Three- and four-word stories start on worksheet 48.

You model how to read the fast way after the children sound out the story words in lessons 40 to 53. In lessons 54 to 74, the children learn the skills they need to make the transition from sounding out to reading the fast way.

Reading Words the Fast Way (Lessons 75–160)

The children identify whole words when they read the fast way. Whole-word reading begins in reading vocabulary at lesson 60. In story 75, the children read sentences the fast way. By lesson 96 in reading vocabulary, the children read most words the fast way. In stories 107 through 160, the children no longer sound out words; but sounding out continues to be used in the correction procedure.

Individual Fluency Checkouts begin at lesson 108. For a Fluency Checkout, each child reads part of the story the fast way. You time the reading. A rate and accuracy criterion is specified.

Comprehension (Lessons 28–160)

Comprehension of reading-vocabulary words begins in lesson 28 with the introduction of "meaning" sentences. Starting at lesson 40, comprehension skills are taught within the story track through the oral questions you present, through discussion of the pictures for the stories, and through written questions on the worksheets.

Pictures. In lessons 40 to 99, the story and the picture related to the story are not on the same page. Children use the words they read to predict something about the content of the picture. Then they look at the picture as you ask questions. At this point in the program, the emphasis is on making sure the children comprehend what they read. They first read the words; then they look at the picture. They do not use "picture cues" to help them figure out words because pictures do not imply specific words.

Oral Questions. From lessons 75 to 160, you ask comprehension questions during the reading of the story. The questions and the points at which they are to be asked are specified. Many questions deal with *who, what, where, when, why,* and *how.* For another type of question, you summarize story events and ask the children to predict what will happen next. For questions that can be answered directly from the words in the story, you signal for a group response. For questions that call for divergent responses—such as, "What do you think?"—you call on individual children.

Written Questions. From lessons 131 to 160, children answer written questions about the story. These questions are on the worksheets.

Read the Items. From lessons 151 to 160, the children play a game called Read the Items. The items are not intuitively obvious, and therefore call for careful teaching and understanding. For example, children read, "If the teacher says 'go,' stand up." To play the game, the children must remember the instructions because you will say different things, such as "stand up" and "go." (Children are to respond only to "go" for this item.)

Additional Skills (Lessons 48–139)

Through a series of exercises in lessons 48 through 139, children learn a set of skills that facilitate their whole-word reading and sentence reading. These exercises include practice in word finding, sentence saying, period finding, quotation finding, question mark finding, reading the title, word practice, and review of troublesome words.

Student Materials for Story Reading

The children's stories for lessons 40 through 90 are in Workbooks A and B. The children's stories for lessons 91 through 160 are in the Storybook.

Every fifth lesson, beginning at lesson 95, has an extra worksheet page on which one of the children's stories is duplicated. You tell the children, "I'll give you a bonus worksheet. That is an extra worksheet for doing a good job." The children color the picture and take the worksheet home.

Two-part stories begin at lesson 140. The second part of a story begins with a summary of what happened during the first part.

How to Conduct Group Story Activities

1. Seat children so that all are close to you and all can see the Presentation Book. Sit so that you can observe whether each child's finger is pointing to the words and can see whether each child's mouth is forming the words.

2. Seat the higher-performing children on the ends of the group. Place the lower-performing children in the middle of the group.

3. Give all children lap boards or large books on which to place their workbook or storybook.

4. Do not allow the children to turn the page to look at the picture until you tell them to turn the page.

5. Each time you give an instruction to point, quickly check to see that each child is pointing appropriately.

6. During reading, make sure that the children look at the words, not at you.

7. Use an audible signal to elicit their responses.

8. Make sure you listen most frequently to the lowest-performing children in the group.

Children Sound Out the Word and Say It Fast

During lessons 40 to 47, the children do not read actual stories; they read two isolated words on their worksheets. The side 1 illustration below presents the words **at** and **am.** The children sound out each word and then say the word fast. Then individual children read one of the words. You model reading the words the fast way. The children use one of the words as a basis for predicting what they will see in a picture on the other side of the worksheet. The children look at the picture and answer some questions that relate to it.

Lesson 43

STORY
EXERCISE 13
Children sound out the first word and say it fast

a. (Pass out Worksheet 43. Do not let the children look at the picture until exercise 17.)

b. (Hold up side 1 of your worksheet. Point to **at** and **am.**) You're going to read these words.

c. Everybody, touch the first ball for the first word. ✔

• Look at the sounds in the word and figure out what you're going to say. (Pause three seconds.)

d. Sound it out. Get ready. (Tap for each sound, pausing about two seconds between taps.) *Children move their finger under each sound as they say aaat.*

e. Again, finger on the first ball. ✔

• Sound it out. Get ready. (Tap for each sound, pausing about two seconds between taps.) *Aaat.*

f. (Repeat *e* until firm.)

g. Everybody, say it fast. (Signal.) *At.* What word? (Signal.) *At.* Yes, **at.**

h. (Repeat *e* and *g* until firm.)

EXERCISE 14
Children sound out the next word and say it fast

a. Everybody, touch the first ball for the next word. ✔

• After you read that word, you'll see a picture for that word. Look at the sounds in the word and figure out what you're going to say. (Pause three seconds.)

b. Sound it out. Get ready. (Tap for each sound, pausing about two seconds between taps.) *Children move their finger under each sound as they say aaammm.*

c. Again, finger on the first ball. ✔

• Sound it out. Get ready. (Tap for each sound, pausing about two seconds between taps.) *Aaammm.*

d. (Repeat *c* until firm.)

e. Everybody, say it fast. (Signal.) *Am.*

• What word? (Signal.) *Am.* Yes, **am.**

f. (Repeat *c* and *e* until firm.)

EXERCISE 15
Individual test

a. Everybody, follow along with your finger as I call on individual children to read one of the words.

b. Everybody, touch the first ball for the first word. ✔

• (Call on a child.) Sound it out. Get ready. (Tap for each sound, pausing about two seconds between taps.) *Aaat.*

• Say it fast. (Signal.) *At.* Yes, **at.**

c. Everybody, touch the first ball for the next word. ✔

• (Call on a child.) Sound it out. Get ready. (Tap for each sound, pausing about two seconds between taps.) *Aaammm.*

• Say it fast. (Signal.) *Am.* Yes, **am.**

d. (Call on individual children to do *b* or *c*.)

EXERCISE 16
Teacher reads the fast way

a. (Hold up your worksheet.)

b. (Touch the first ball of the arrow for **am.**) Everybody, I'm going to read this word the fast way. (Slash as you say:) **am.** I read it the fast way.

c. (Touch the first ball of the arrow for **am.**) I'll read it again. (Slash as you say:) **am.**

EXERCISE 17
Picture comprehension

a. You've read the word (pause) **am.** Now you're going to see a picture. The picture will show who I really . . . (Signal.) *Am.* Yes, **am.**

b. Everybody, turn your worksheet over and look at the picture. ✔

c. (Ask these questions:)

1. Is that who I really am? *The children respond.*

• No, that's not who I am.

2. Who is that in the picture? *The children respond.*

• Yes, a big, mean tiger.

3. Am I really a big, mean tiger? *The children respond.*

4. What would you do if you had that big, mean tiger? *The children respond.*

Worksheet, Side 1

Worksheet, Side 2

Exercise 13 Teaching Techniques

- *Step a.* Do not let the children look at the picture until exercise 17. You want them to read the word before they relate it to the picture. Enforce this rule.
- *Step c.* Be sure that the children figure out the sounds in the word **at** before sounding it out. If the children are not obviously attending to the sounds, tell them to move under each sound and say it to themselves. Pause at least three seconds before beginning the sounding out. This pause is critical to give the children time to look at the sounds.
- *Step d.* Pause about two seconds between taps. Check to see that the children are touching under each sound as you tap. (They practiced this behavior on worksheets 19 to 33.) The children are not to stop between the sounds when they say them.
- *Step e.* Be sure that the children are touching the first ball for **at.**
- *Step g.* Give an audible signal—a tap or a snap—for the children to say the word fast. They must be looking at their papers, not at you.

Exercises 15–17 Teaching Techniques

- *Exercise 15.* Check to see that all the children are following along with their fingers as individual children read one of the words. You may have to move some children's fingers.
- *Exercise 16.* Be sure the children are looking at your worksheet as you model how to read the word the fast way.
- *Exercise 17, step a.* Be sure the children are looking at you.
- *Exercise 17, step c.* The children should be looking at the picture. Do not signal. Let individual children respond. But do not let the discussion continue for more than about ten seconds.

Corrections

Correct sound misidentification by telling (modeling) the correct sound and repeating the step in which the mistake occurred.

Correct touching errors by physically moving the children's fingers and repeating the step. If children stop between the sounds, present a model by calling on an individual to sound out the word.

If children cannot say a word fast, correct as you did in reading vocabulary (page 35) by changing the exercise into an oral exercise. Then direct the children to sound out and identify the word on their worksheet.

Remember to follow each correction with a repetition of the step that was missed.

Below are a series of correction procedures for word-identification errors on group reading or on individual tests. If you compare the procedures, you'll see that they are similar to each other, with only slight variations. For group reading, the last step in the correction in lessons 40 to 47 involves repeating the **word** that was missed. In lessons 48 to 160, it involves repeating the **sentence** that was missed.

Similarly, for an individual test, in lessons 40 to 93, the last step in the correction involves repeating the **word** that was missed, while in lessons 94 to 160, the last step involves repeating the **sentence** that was missed.

Learn these correction procedures and refer back to them as you work through the story formats in this guide.

Group Reading (Lessons 40–47)
Correction for Word-Identification Errors

The correction involves the following steps:

1. Identifying the word

2. Directing the group to sound out and identify the word

3. Repeating the steps for sounding out the word

The group is reading the word **at** (lesson 43, exercise 13, steps *e* to *g*). Jim and Ed make mistakes at step 4.

1. Teacher: Again, finger on the first ball. ✔ Sound it out. Get ready. (Tap for each sound, pausing about two seconds between taps.)
2. Group: *Aaat.*
3. Teacher: Everybody, say it fast. (Signal.)
4. Jim: *Aaa.*
   Terry: *At.*
   Ed: *It.*
5. Teacher: That word is **at.** Everybody, finger on the ball. ✔ Sound it out. Get ready. (Tap for each sound, pausing about two seconds between taps.)
6. Group: *Aaat.*
7. Teacher: Everybody, say it fast. (Signal.)
8. Group: *At.*
9. Teacher: What word? (Signal.)
10. Group: *At.*
11. Teacher: Yes, **at.** Good. You said it fast. Starting over. (Return to step *e* and present steps *e* through *g.*)

Individual Test (Lessons 40–93)
Correction for Word-Identification Errors

The correction involves the following steps:

1. Identifying the word

2. Directing the group to sound out and identify the word

3. After giving other children individual tests, requiring the child who made the mistake to sound out the word and identify it

Individual test on the word **am** (lesson 43, exercise 15, step c). Lola makes a mistake at step 4.

1. Teacher: Everybody, touch the first ball for the next word. ✔
   Lola, sound it out. Get ready. (Tap for each sound, pausing about two seconds between taps.)
2. Lola: *Aaammm.*
3. Teacher: Say it fast. (Signal.)
4. Lola: At.
5. Teacher: That word is **am. Everybody, finger on the ball.** ✔
   Sound it out. Get ready. (Tap for each sound, pausing about two seconds between taps.)
6. Group: *Aaammm.*
7. Teacher: Everybody, say it fast. (Signal.)
8. Group: *Am.*
9. Teacher: Yes, **am.** (Continue with exercise 15. After completing exercise 15, return to Lola.)
10. Teacher: (Point to the ball for **am.**) Lola, touch the ball for this word. ✔
    Sound it out. Get ready. (Tap for each sound, pausing about two seconds between taps.)
11. Lola: *Aaammm.*
12. Teacher: Say it fast. (Signal.)
13. Lola: *Am.*
14. Teacher: Yes, **am.** Good. You said it fast.

Group Reading (Lessons 48–160)
Correction for Word-Identification Errors

Worksheet 48

The correction involves returning to the beginning of the sentence and rereading the sentence. Here are the steps:

1. Identify the word. That word is . . .

2. Direct the group to sound out and identify the word. Everybody, sound it out. Get ready . . . What word?

3. Direct the group to return to the first word of the sentence and read the entire sentence. Starting over, or Back to the first word (of the sentence).

Until the words **period** and **sentence** have been taught, you will have to show the children where to start rereading.

Individual Test (Lessons 94–160)
Correction for Word-Identification Errors

Story 94

a littl₌ fish sat on a fat fish.

The correction involves returning to the beginning of the sentence and rereading the sentence. Here are the steps:

1. Identify the word. That word is . . .

2. Direct the group to sound out and identify the word. Everybody, sound it out. Get ready . . . What word?

3. Require the child who made the mistake to sound out the word and identify it. Sound it out. Get ready . . . What word?

4. Direct the child to return to the first word of the sentence and read the entire sentence. Back to the first word of the sentence.

The words **sentence** and **period** have been taught by lesson 94.

Sounding Out Words Track Development

Boxes Between the Words (Lessons 48–86)

Three- and four-word stories begin in lesson 48. Boxes on the line between the words keep the children from running the words together. You establish the terminology of "first word" and "next word" by having the children touch the beginning ball for the first word and sound the word out. Then they touch the box for the next word and sound it out.

Worksheet 49

Starting at lesson 56, there are no balls under the sounds in the words, but you continue to tap for each sound and the children continue to touch under the sounds. The stories get longer in lessons 61 to 86, and the boxes move above the line and gradually get smaller until they are phased out in lesson 87.

Teacher and Children Read the Fast Way (Lessons 54–74)

In lessons 40 to 53, you modeled how to read the fast way after the children sounded out the words in the story. In lessons 54 to 74, you and the children read part of the story the fast way. You provide a strong model of inflection and whole-word reading. The lower-performing children, especially, need this strong model; so be sure to teach these exercises to criterion.

Lesson 57

EXERCISE 16

Teacher and children read the fast way

a. (Point to the words on the first arrow. Touch under **on.**) Everybody, this word is (pause) **on.** What word? (Signal.) On.
• Yes, **on.** Remember that.
b. We're going to read this story the fast way.
c. (Point to **it is.**) I'll read these words the fast way.
d. (Point to **on.**) When I touch this word, you're going to say . . . (Signal.) On. Yes, **on.**
e. (Repeat *d* until firm.)
f. (Touch the ball of the arrow.) Reading the fast way. (Pause three seconds. Touch under **it is** and say:) It is . . .
g. (Then touch under **on.**) On.
h. (Repeat *f* and *g* until firm.)
i. Yes, **it is on.**

Worksheet 57

• *Step a.* After you ask, "What word?" move to the end of the arrow. The children should respond *on.*

• *Step d.* Signal the children to complete the sentence. Watch your voice cue and your timing. Say, "When I touch this word, you're going to saaaaaay. . . ." and move to the end of the arrow.

• *Step f.* After you say, "Reading the fast way," be sure to pause for three seconds. Move quickly to **it** and say **it.** (If you move slowly, the children may try to respond with you.) Then move quickly to **is** and say **is.**

• *Step g.* Move more slowly to **on.** Children are to respond the instant you stop under the word, not before.

• Repeat steps *f* and *g* until the children are firm. Then say, "Yes, it is on."

Correction

Use this correction procedure for step g if the children begin to sound out the word instead of saying it fast.

model ——→ **1.** Immediately say the word **on**

lead ——→ **2.** Repeat steps *f* and *g,* responding with the children at step *g.* Repeat the lead.

test ——→ **3.** Repeat step *f.* Then present step *g.* Do not respond with the children.

delayed

test ——→ **4.** Say, "Let's do it again." Return to step *a* and present the format. Do not lead the children at step *g.*

Dotted Arrows Between the Lines
(Lessons 61–74)

Beginning with lesson 61, the stories are printed on two lines.

Worksheet 61

The dotted arrow from the first line to the second line is a prompt for the children. Some children have a tendency to go from the end of the first line to the end of the second line. The dotted arrow prompts children to begin the next line at the left. The dotted arrow is dropped at lesson 75, after the children have mastered the convention of proceeding from line to line.

EXERCISE 18

Children follow the arrow to the bottom line

a. (Pass out Worksheet 61. Do not let the children look at the picture until exercise 22.)

b. (Point to the story.) These words are on two lines. Watch me touch all the words.

c. (Touch **this** and **is.**) Now I follow the arrow to the ball on the next line. (Follow the arrow.)

d. Now I touch the rest of the words. (Touch **not** and **me.**)

e. (Repeat *b* through *d* two times.)

f. Your turn. Finger on the ball of the <u>top</u> line. ✔

g. Touch the words when I tap. Get ready. (Tap for **this** and **is.**) *The children respond.*

h. Now follow the arrow to the next ball. ✔

i. (Repeat *f* through *h* until firm.)

j. Touch the words on the bottom line when I tap. Get ready. (Tap for **not** and **me.**) *The children respond.*

k. This time you're going to touch all the words in the story. Finger on the ball of the <u>top</u> line. ✔

• Get ready. (Tap for **this** and **is.**)

l. (Do not tap for **not** until the children have followed the arrow to the ball on the bottom line. Then tap for **not** and **me.**)

m. (Repeat *k* and *l* until firm.)

• *Step f.* Be sure to refer to the first line as the <u>top</u> line and stress the word **top.** You are using the word <u>first</u> in connection with **first word** and **first sound.**

• *Step g.* The children may start to sound out the word rather than pointing and touching. Stress the word **touch.** Repeat step *g* until students touch without sounding out the word.

• *Step l.* If the children do not move their finger to the ball of the second line, you may have to tell them, "Go to the next ball," or "Follow the arrow to the next ball." Remember to present the delayed test after any corrections. Repeat steps *k* and *l* until firm.

Throughout the word-reading activities in the reading-vocabulary and story tracks, the emphasis is on increasing the children's ability to decode without sounding out words. The steps that lead to whole-word reading are sequenced so that the children are able to relate the attack skill of sounding out words to the skill of remembering words. Children do not lose the sounding-out ability. They simply add the ability to remember words. This combination gives them the tools they need to figure out new words and the strategy they need to note the details of words and remember them.

Lesson 75

Do not tap for any small letters.

EXERCISE 20

First reading—children sound out each word and tell what word

a. (Pass out Worksheet 75. Do not let the children look at the picture until exercise 22.)

b. Get ready to read the story. First word. ✔

c. Get ready. (Tap for each sound.) *Hēēē.*
- What word? (Signal.) *He.* Yes, **he.**

d. Next word. ✔

e. Get ready. (Tap for each sound.) *Āāāt.*
- What word? (Signal.) *Ate.* Yes, **ate.**

f. (Repeat *d* and *e* for the remaining words in the story.)

EXERCISE 21

Second reading—children reread the story and answer questions

a. This time you'll read the story and I'll ask questions. Back to the first word. ✔

b. (Repeat *c* through *f* in exercise 20. Ask the comprehension questions below as the children read.)

After the children read:	You say:
He ate a fig.	What did he eat? (Signal.) *A fig.*
And he is sick.	How does he feel? (Signal.) *Sick.* Why? (Signal.) *Because he ate a fig.*

To Correct

(If the children do not give acceptable answers, have them reread the sentence that answers the question. Then ask the question again.)

EXERCISE 22

Picture comprehension

a. What do you think you are going to see in the picture? *The children respond.*

b. Turn your worksheet over and look at the picture.

c. (Ask these questions:)
1. Is he eating a fig? *The children respond.* No.
2. Why is he sick? *The children respond.* He ate a fig.
3. What is that thing in his mouth? *The children respond.* A thermometer.
4. What's the doctor going to do to make him feel better? *The children respond.*

EXERCISE 23

Word finding

a. Turn your worksheet back to side 1. Everybody, look at the words in the top line. One of the words is **he.**

b. Get ready to touch **he** when I tap. (Pause three seconds.) Get ready. (Clap.) *The children touch* **hē.**

c. (Repeat *b* for these words: **fig, hē, āte, fig, āte, fig, hē, āte, hē, fig, atē.**)

EXERCISE 24

Children read the first sentence the fast way

a. Everybody, now you're going to read part of the story the fast way. Finger on the ball of the top line. ✔

b. Move your finger under the sounds of the first word and figure out the sounds you're going to say. Don't say the sounds out loud. Just figure out what you're going to say. ✔
- (Prompt children who don't touch under the sounds. Pause five seconds.) Read the word the fast way. Get ready. (Tap. Say **he** with the children.) *He.*

c. Next word. Move your finger under the sounds and figure out the sounds. ✔
- (Pause five seconds.) Read the word the fast way. Get ready. (Tap. Say **ate** with the children.) *Ate.*

d. (Repeat *c* for the words **a, fig.**)

e. Let's read the words the fast way again. Everybody, finger on the ball of the top line. ✔
- Figure out the first word and get ready to read it the fast way. Say the sounds to yourself. (Pause five seconds.) What word? (Tap.) *He.* Yes, **he.**

f. Figure out the next word. Say the sounds to yourself. (Pause five seconds.) What word? (Tap.) *Ate.* Yes, **ate.**

g. (Repeat *f* for the words **a, fig.**)

EXERCISE 25

Individual test

a. Everybody, finger on the ball of the top line. ✔

b. We're going to have different children read. Everybody's going to touch the words.

c. Everybody, touch the first word. ✔

d. (Call on a child.) Reading the fast way. Get ready. (Tap.) *He.*

e. Next word. ✔

f. Everybody reading. Get ready. (Tap.) *Ate.*

g. Next word. ✔

h. (Call on a child.) Get ready. (Tap.) *A.*

i. (Repeat *e* and *f* for **fig.**)

Worksheet 75, Side 1

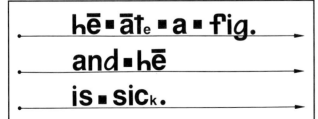

Worksheet 75, Side2

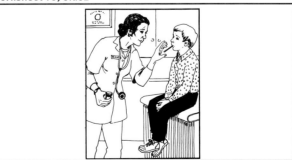

Reading the Fast Way, Lesson 75

Starting with lesson 75, a number of changes appear in the procedures for reading the worksheet story. On the first reading of the story, the children use familiar procedures to sound out each word one time and tell what word.

On the second reading of the story, you ask questions at specified points in the reading.

After the second reading, the children look at the picture, and you ask questions about it.

Next, the children play word finding with three words that appear in the top line of the story.

Then, the children read the first sentence the fast way—a new activity.

Finally, you present a new format for individual turns. You intersperse group reading and individual reading.

Exercise 20. Sounding Out Words That Begin with Stop Sounds

The children sound out each word only one time before they identify the word. Before lesson 67 you tapped for each sound, pausing two seconds between taps as the children hold each sound. But the word **hē** begins with a stop sound, and there is no way the children can hold a stop sound until they say the sound that follows. If you pause two seconds between taps, the children must either pause between the stop sound and the next sound or mispronounce the stop sound. To guide the sounding out, you must tap for **h** and then quickly for **ēēē**. Children should not stop between the sounds as they say . . .

Children: hēēē

Note that the children say both sounds in response to your second tap.

For the word **him,** you would tap for **h**; tap quickly for **iii** as the children say **hiii**; and tap quickly for **mmm.**

Exercise 23. Word Finding

Word-finding activities started at lesson 57 as a transition activity between sounding out words and reading words the fast way.

In lesson 75, exercise 23, an abbreviated form of the activity is presented.

- *Step a.* Make sure that children are looking at the words and not at you or at their neighbor's story.
- *Step b.* Make sure they are pointing to the appropriate word before you signal.
- *Step c.* Present the series until the children are firm.

Correction

If the child touches a wrong word, have the child sound out and identify that word.
Sound out the word you're touching.
Get ready . . . What word?
Is that the word **fig?**
Look for the word **fig, ffffiiig.**

Exercise 24. Children Read the First Sentence the Fast Way

This is a new kind of reading exercise. Children reread the first sentence the fast way. <u>You tap one time for each word.</u>

- *Step b.* If children don't move their fingers under the sounds, guide their fingers.

    Pause five seconds before saying, "Read the word the fast way." Count to yourself or tap your foot five times. You must pause long enough before saying, "Get ready," to allow the children to figure out the word. Some children will audibly sound out the word as they point to the sounds. This behavior is quite acceptable. If the children sound out too loudly, tell them to whisper. But allow them to go through the familiar steps of sounding the word out.

    Say, "Get ready," tap, and say **he** with the children.

- *Steps c and d.* Repeat the procedures for the remaining words in the first sentence.
- *Step e.* Note that you ask, "What word?" and tap, but you do *not* lead by saying the word with the children. You reinforce by saying, "Yes, **he.**"
- *Steps f and g.* Repeat the procedures for the remaining words in the first sentence.

Correction

Use the same correction procedure you used for word-identification errors on page 48.

Reading the Fast Way Track Development

In lessons 75 to 86, the children read the first sentence the fast way.

In lesson 87, the children are taught to find the periods and to say a sentence.

In lessons 87 to 90, the children read the first two sentences the fast way.

In lesson 91, the children reread the entire story the fast way.

In lessons 107 to 160, the children read the story the fast way on the first reading.

Reading Sentences the Fast Way, Lesson 87

Lesson 87

EXERCISE 20
Period finding

a. Turn your worksheet back to side 1. Everybody, we're going to read all the words in the first sentence the fast way.

b. (Point to the first word.) The first <u>sentence</u> begins here and goes all the way to a little dot called a period. So I just go along the arrow until I find a period.

c. (Touch **shē**.) Have I come to a period yet? (Signal.) *No.*
(Touch **is**.) Have I come to a period yet? (Signal.) *No.*
(Touch **in**.) Have I come to a period yet? (Signal.) *No.*
(Touch **thē**.) Have I come to a period yet? (Signal.) *No.*
(Touch **rāin**.) Have I come to a period yet? (Signal.) *Yes.*

d. Again. (Repeat *b* and *c* until firm.)

e. Everybody, put your finger on the ball of the top line. ✔

f. Get ready to find the period for the first sentence. Go along the arrow until you find that period. ✔

EXERCISE 21
Children read the first sentence the fast way

a. Everybody, get ready to read all the words in the first sentence the fast way.

b. Touch the first word. ✔
• (Pause three seconds.) Get ready. (Tap.) *She.*

c. Next word. ✔
• (Pause three seconds.) Get ready. (Tap.) *Is.*

d. (Repeat *c* for the words **in, thē, rāin**.)

e. (After the children read **rain** say:) Stop. That's the end of the sentence.

f. Let's read that sentence again, the fast way.

g. First word. ✔
• Get ready. (Tap.) *She.*

h. Next word. ✔
• Get ready. (Tap.) *Is.*

i. (Repeat *h* for the words **in, thē, rāin**.)

j. (After the children read **rain** say:) Stop. You've read the first sentence.

EXERCISE 22
Children read the second sentence the fast way

a. Everybody, put your finger on the period after **rāin**. ✔

b. Now move along the arrows until you find the next period. ✔

c. (Repeat *a* and *b* until firm.)

d. Put your finger on the period after **rāin**. ✔

e. Get ready to read all the words until we come to the next period.

f. Starting with the first word after **rāin**. ✔ (Pause three seconds.) Get ready. (Tap.) *She.*

g. Next word. ✔ (Pause three seconds.) Get ready. (Tap.) *Has.*

h. (Repeat *g* for the remaining words in the second sentence.)

i. (After the children read **sack** say:) Stop. You've read the sentence.

j. Let's read it again. Go back to the period after **rāin**.✔
Get ready to read all the words in the sentence.

k. First word. ✔
Get ready. (Tap.) *She.*

l. Next word. ✔
Get ready. (Tap.) *Has.*

m. (Repeat *l* for the remaining words in the second sentence.)

EXERCISE 24
Sentence saying

Good reading. Now, everybody, say all the words in that sentence without looking. (Signal.) *The children repeat the sentence at a normal speaking rate.* Yes, she is in the rain.

Exercise 20. Period Finding

In exercise 20, you introduce the words **period** and **first sentence.** In exercise 21, steps *e* and *j*, you tell the children that they have come to the end of the sentence. After you have presented these two exercises for several lessons, the children will understand the relationship between a period and a sentence.

Exercise 21. Children Read the First Sentence the Fast Way

• *Step b.* Practice the timing. Say, "Touch the first word." Scan the children's pointing fingers. Watch their mouths forming the words. Pause three seconds. Say, "Get ready." Tap.

• *Steps c and d.* As soon as the children respond, say, "Next word" . . . Scan . . . Pause three seconds . . . Say, "Get ready" . . . Tap.

• *Steps g and h.* Continue to use the three-second pause, although it is not specified.

Exercise 22. Children Read the Second Sentence the Fast Way

Maintain your three-second pause in steps *f* through *h* before you tap for each word. Reduce the length of the pause in steps *j* through *m*.

• *Step j.* A signal is not specified for finding a period. The reason is that all children cannot be expected to find the period at the same time. Some children will move along the line faster than others. In the first few presentations, you may have to tell the children, "Go ahead. Do it."

Exercise 24. Sentence Saying

This exercise requires children to remember the words in a sentence. They should say the sentence at a normal, brisk pace with an inflection that conveys the meaning of the sentence. The group should repeat the sentence until all words are properly sequenced and the inflection is appropriate.

If a child omits a word, says the words out of sequence, or inflects inappropriately, repeat the sentence. Then have the children repeat the sentence.

Additional Sentence-Reading Activities

At lesson 94 you introduce quotations; the children answer questions on the first and second reading of the story; and individual children read whole sentences the fast way.

Quotation Finding

Lesson 94

EXERCISE 24

Quotation finding

a. (Pass out Storybook.)
b. Open your book to page 7. ✔
c. (Point to the quotation marks around the word **wow** in the second sentence.) These marks show that somebody is saying something. He's saying the word between these marks.
d. (Point to the quotation marks around **that fat fish is mom** in the last sentence.) These marks show that somebody is saying something. He's saying all the words between these marks.
e. (Point to the quotation marks around **wow**.) Everybody, touch these marks in your story. ✔
• Somebody is saying the word between those marks.
f. (Point to the quotation marks around **that fat fish is mom**.) Everybody, touch these marks in your story. ✔
• Somebody is saying all the words between those marks.
g. (Repeat e and f until firm.)

Story 94

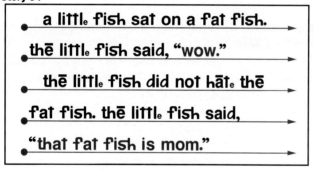

a little fish sat on a fat fish.

the little fish said, "wow."

the little fish did not hate the

fat fish. the little fish said,

"that fat fish is mom."

Quotations are in red type in the first several stories. The sentence-saying practice has prepared the children for repeating what is said within quotation marks.

• *Steps c and d.* Be sure that you show the children the quotation marks and the word or words between the marks. You can point with two fingers to the set of quotation marks, or you may want to prop the book so you can point to the marks with both hands.

When you refer to the words "between the marks," run a finger under the word or words to which you refer.

• *Steps e and f.* Do not signal. Watch to make sure that the children touch the marks. You may have to help them by placing their index fingers on the quotation marks.

Answering Questions

Lesson 94

EXERCISE 25

First reading—children read the story and answer questions

a. You're going to read the story and I'll ask questions.
b. (Tap for the sounds in each word as the children sound out each word one time and tell what word. Present the items below as the children read.)

After the children read:	You say:
The little fish said,	Now we're going to read what he said.
"Wow."	What did the little fish say? (Signal.) *Wow.*
The little fish said,	Now we're going to read what he said.
"That fat fish is Mom."	What did he say? (Signal.) *That fat fish is Mom.*

If the children do not respond on signal at a normal speaking rate, correct by presenting a model, and then a test, as you did for sentence saying on page 53. Then present a delayed test by asking the question again.

Individual Children Read a Sentence the Fast Way

Lesson 94

EXERCISE 28

Individual test

a. I'm going to call on individual children to read a whole sentence the fast way. Everybody's going to touch the words.
b. First word of the story. ✔
• (Call on a child to read the first sentence. Do not tap for each word.)
c. (Call on a child to read the second sentence. Do not tap for each word.)

• Individual children read at their own rate; you do not tap. Other children follow along.
• Praise children who read rapidly and accurately. Praise children who read with inflection. Praise children who are trying hard and doing well.
• Provide several individual tests. Be sure to call on some lower-performing children.

Lesson 98

> **EXERCISE 18**
>
> First reading—question mark finding
>
> (Have the children reread any sentences containing words that give them trouble. Keep a list of these words.)
> **a.** (Pass out Storybook.)
> **b.** Open your book to page 15 and get ready to read. ✔
> **c.** (Tap for the sounds in each word of the first sentence as the children sound out each word one time and tell what word.)
> **d.** (After the children read **shē was not mad at him,** say:) Everybody, move along the lines until you come to the next period. Oh, oh. There's no period in this sentence. There's a funny mark called a question mark.
> **e.** Everybody, touch the question mark. ✔
> **f.** There's a question mark in this sentence because this sentence asks a question. Everybody, get ready to read the question.
> **g.** Finger on the first word. ✔
> • (Tap for the sounds in each word of the sentence as the children sound out each word one time and tell what word.)
> **h.** (After the children read **did shē hit him?** say:) Everybody, say that question. *The children repeat the question at a normal speaking rate.*
> **i.** Yes, **did shē hit him?** Let's read the next sentence and find out.
> **j.** Finger on the first word. ✔
> • (Tap for the sounds in each word of the sentence as the children sound out each word one time and tell what word.)
> **k.** Did she hit him? (Signal.) *No.*
> **l.** Everybody, get ready to read the next sentence. (Repeat *g* through *k* for the sentences: **did shē hug him? nō, nō, nō.**)
> **m.** Everybody, get ready to read the next sentence. (Repeat *g* and *h* for the last sentence: **did shē kiss him?**)
> **n.** Did she kiss him? We'll find out later.
> **o.** (After the first reading of the story, print on the board the words that the children missed more than one time. Have the children sound out each word one time and tell what word.)
> **p.** (After the group's responses are firm, call on individual children to read the words.)

Story 98

> shē was not mad at him. did
> shē hit him? nō, nō, nō. did shē
> hug him? nō, nō, nō. did shē
> kiss him?

This format teaches the difference between the question mark and the period. The children read each question in the story, say the question at a normal speaking rate, and read the answer.

Children Read the Fast Way Without Sounding Out
(Lessons 107–160)

Major changes take place during these lessons. The children no longer sound out during story reading except as a correction. During group story reading, the group reads the fast way. Individual children read sentences. You present individual Fluency Checkouts and time each child reading the whole story or part of the story without sounding out.

Lesson 108

> **EXERCISE 20**
>
> First reading—children read the story the fast way
>
> (Have the children reread any sentences containing words that give them trouble. Keep a list of these words.)
> **a.** (Pass out Storybook.)
> **b.** Open your book to page 37 and get ready to read. ✔
> **c.** We're going to read this story the fast way.
> **d.** Touch the first word. ✔
> **e.** Reading the fast way. First word. (Pause three seconds.) Get ready. (Tap.) *Thē.*
> **f.** Next word. ✔
> • (Pause three seconds.) Get ready. (Tap.) *Old.*
> **g.** (Repeat *f* for the remaining words in the first sentence. Pause at least three seconds between taps. The children are to identify each word without sounding it out.)
> **h.** (Repeat *d* through *g* for the next two sentences. Have the children reread the first three sentences until firm.)
> **i.** (The children are to read the remainder of the story the fast way, stopping at the end of each sentence.)
> **j.** (After the first reading of the story, print on the board the words that the children missed more than one time. Have the children sound out each word one time and tell what word.)
> **k.** (After the group's responses are firm, call on individual children to read the words.)

Story 108

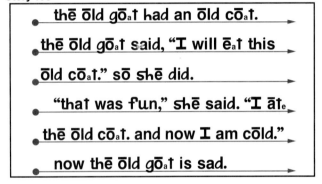

> thē ōld gōₐt had an ōld cōₐt.
> thē ōld gōₐt said, "I will ēₐt this
> ōld cōₐt." sō shē did.
> "that was fun," shē said. "I āte
> thē ōld cōₐt. and now I am cōld."
> now thē ōld gōₐt is sad.

• Keep a list of troublesome words for word practices at steps *j* and *k*.
• *Steps b through g.* These procedures are similar to those you used for reading the fast way in lessons 87 to 106. (See page 53.)
• *Step h.* You direct the reading and rereading of the first three sentences until the children are firm. Pause at least three seconds before signaling for each word. If the children are firm at reading one word every three seconds, they will be likely to maintain their rate through the rest of the story.

 Note that the children reread any sentences that are not firm. Some children will have difficulty reading the fast way at this specified rate. You can pause longer than three seconds before words that you know might take longer to figure out, such as new words, words beginning with a stop sound, or words children had trouble with during the reading-vocabulary exercises.

The simplest way to determine an appropriate rate for group reading is to direct individual children to read the passage. Note the amount of time each child requires for different words. Based on their performance, adjust the timing of your signal so that it is slow enough for about eighty percent of the children's individual performances. If some children are consistently very slow (requiring more than five seconds per word), provide additional firming before proceeding in the program.

- *Step i.* Children are to stop at the end of each sentence. On the second reading you will ask questions at the end of some sentences.

Procedures for Lessons 115 to 160
Beginning with story 115, the stories have titles. In the first story exercise for lessons 115 through 118, you hold up your storybook, point to the title, and say, "These words are called the title of the story. These words tell what the story is about . . . What is this story about?"

Lesson 119

EXERCISE 19

First reading—children read the story the fast way

(Have the children reread any sentences containing words that give them trouble. Keep a list of these words.)

a. (Pass out Storybook.)
b. Open your book to page 68. ✔
c. Everybody, touch the title of the story and get ready to read the words in the title the fast way.
d. First word. ✔
- (Pause two seconds.) Get ready. (Tap.) *Al.*
e. (Tap for each remaining word in the title.)
f. (After the children have read the title, ask:) What's this story about? (Signal.) *Al and Sal.* Yes, **Al and Sal.**
g. Everybody, get ready to read this story the fast way.
h. First word. ✔
- (Pause two seconds.) Get ready. (Tap.) *Al.*
i. (Tap for the remaining words in the first sentence. Pause at least two seconds between taps.)
j. (Repeat *h* and *i* for the next two sentences. Have the children reread the first three sentences until firm.)
k. (The children are to read the remainder of the story the fast way, stopping at the end of each sentence.)
l. (After the first reading of the story, print on the board the words that the children missed more than one time. Have the children sound out each word one time and tell what word.)
m. (After the group's responses are firm, call on individual children to read the words.)

---

al and sal →

al said, "will wē gō hōme?" →

sal said, "nō. wē will gō to that farm." →

al said, "will wē have fun on that →
farm?" →

sal said, "wē can run with a cow. →

wē can ēat cōrn. wē can fēēd pigs. wē →
can sit in the lāke." →

al said, "I hāte to sit in lākes." →

sō sal and al did not sit in the lāke. →

sal and al had fun with the pigs. →

- *Step h.* Some children may touch the first word of the title instead of the first word of the story. Firm the discrimination by telling the children, "You're not touching the first word of the story." Hold up your storybook and touch the first word of the story. "Here's the first word of the story. Everybody, touch it . . . Listen: Everybody, touch the first word of the title. Get ready . . . Listen: Everybody, touch the first word of the story. Get ready . . ."

- *Step i.* Here are some guidelines for tapping:
  (1) Slow the pace for the first word in every line after the first line. Do this by saying, "Next word," as soon as the children read the last word of a line. Then say, "Get ready . . ." Tap. Make sure that the children are touching under the first word of the line before you tap for the words.
  (2) Slow the pace before troublesome words.
  (3) Use the individual tests and individual Fluency Checkouts to determine whether the children are reading the words in the group reading or are being led. If their rates on individual tests or Fluency Checkouts are typically slower than the rate you establish for the group reading, your rate is too fast. If they make a number of errors on individual tests, they are probably being led during the group reading.

(4) Make sure that children point under the words that are being read—both on group and individual turns. Watch the children's mouths as they form the words and observe whether they are pointing appropriately.

(5) Except for words that are preceded by "Get ready . . ." all words must be presented at a constant rate. The children benefit by knowing how much time they have to prepare the next word and the rate at which you expect them to read.

Individual Children or the Group Read Sentences on the First Reading (Lessons 140–160)

Lesson 140

> **EXERCISE 21**
>
> Individual children or the group read sentences to complete the first reading
>
> **a.** I'm going to call on individual children to read a sentence. Everybody, follow along and point to the words. If you hear a mistake, raise your hand.
> **b.** (Call on a child.) Read the next sentence. (Do not tap for the words. Let children read at their own pace, but be sure they read the sentence correctly.)
>
> **To Correct**
> (Have the child sound out the word. Then return to the beginning of the sentence.)
>
> **c.** (Repeat *b* for most of the remaining sentences in the story. Occasionally have the group read a sentence. When the group is to read, say:) Everybody, read the next sentence. (Pause two seconds.) Get ready. (Tap for each word in the sentence. Pause at least two seconds between taps.)

After the group is firm on the title and the first three sentences, you call on individual children to read a sentence. Intersperse some group turns. Children raise their hand if they hear a mistake. Use the corrections on page 48 to correct the group or the individual.

INDIVIDUAL FLUENCY CHECKOUTS: RATE/ACCURACY (Lessons 108–160)

Individual Fluency Checkouts begin after the children have learned to read stories the fast way on the first reading. Fluency Checkouts appear in lessons 108, 109, 110, and in every fifth lesson until the end of the program. The Fluency Checkouts are presented to the children individually. They are very important for both the children and for you. For the children, they provide practice in reading a long passage the fast way. The Fluency Checkouts also demonstrate to the children that they are to use the strategy of reading the fast way and are not to continue sounding out words.

For you, the Fluency Checkouts provide information about the children's progress. This information is not a duplication of the mastery-test information. The Fluency Checkouts show you in detail whether the children are progressing acceptably, whether additional firming is needed, whether children tend to make particular mistakes you hadn't observed, and whether individuals should be placed in a different part of the program.

To pass a Fluency Checkout, a child must read a selection within a specified period of time and must make no more than three (or four) errors. The length of the selections and the time vary from Fluency Checkout to Fluency Checkout, but these details are specified in the Fluency Checkout instructions.

Make a permanent chart with children's names and lesson numbers for recording the results of individual Fluency Checkouts. A sample chart is shown below.

SAMPLE INDIVIDUAL FLUENCY CHECKOUT: RATE/ACCURACY CHART

Name	Lessons												
	108	109	110	115	120	125	130	135	140	145	150	155	160
Carol	★★	★											
David	★	★	★										
Joan		★★	★										
Kim	★		★★										
Raúl	★★	★★											

Below is a format from lesson 108. It describes the Fluency Checkout procedure.

Lesson 108

> ★**INDIVIDUAL CHECKOUT: STORYBOOK**
>
> **EXERCISE 25**
>
> 2½–minute individual fluency checkout: rate/accuracy—whole story
>
> (Make a permanent chart for recording results of individual checkouts. See Teacher's Guide for sample chart.)
>
> **a.** As you are doing your worksheet, I'll call on children one at a time to read the **whole story.** If you can read the whole story the fast way in less than two and a half minutes and if you make no more than three errors, I'll put two stars after your name on the chart for lesson 108.
>
> **b.** If you make too many errors or don't read the story in less than two and a half minutes, you'll have to practice it and do it again. When you do read it in under two and a half minutes with no more than three errors, you'll get one star. Remember, two stars if you can do it the first time, one star if you do it the second or third time you try.
>
> **c.** (Call on a child. Tell the child:) Read the whole story very carefully the fast way. Go. (Time the child. If the child makes a mistake, quickly tell the child the correct word and permit the child to continue reading. As soon as the child makes more than three errors or exceeds the time limit, tell the child to stop.) You'll have to read the story to yourself and try again later. (Plan to monitor the child's practice.)
>
> **d.** (Record two stars for each child who reads appropriately. Congratulate those children.)
>
> **e.** (Give children who do not earn two stars a chance to read the story again before the next lesson is presented. Award one star to each of those children who meet the rate and accuracy criterion.)
>
> 41 words/**2.5 min** = 16 wpm [**3 errors**]

If more than one-third of the children in the group fail to pass the third Fluency Checkout (lesson 110), you should carefully examine your teaching procedures because the children are not performing acceptably. Pay particular attention to the way you present all reading-vocabulary tasks, and make sure that you are presenting a sufficient number of individuals turns to the lower performers in the group. Also, consider placing the children who do not pass the Fluency Checkouts on the first trial in a group that is at an earlier lesson in the program.

If children make more than three errors and do not complete the Fluency Checkout selection in the specified time, do not work on reading rate. Work on accuracy, and do not hurry the children to try to read fast. Simply give them a lot more practice at reading accurately. As their accuracy improves, praise them when they read faster, but make it very clear that they are to read accurately.

If children make errors because they are trying to read fast, tell them to slow down. The rates that are specified for Fluency Checkouts should be easily attained by the children without rushing. Remember, the first priority is accuracy; rate will follow with practice and reinforcement.

READ THE ITEMS (Lessons 151–160)

Read the items is a vehicle for teaching and testing comprehension skills. The items the children read are designed so that the children must read every word and remember the instructions given in the item. The exercises are presented so that you can test the children to make certain that they are reading carefully and comprehending. Lessons 151 to 154 have only one item. Lessons 155 to 160 have two items.

Lesson 152

> **EXERCISE 23**
>
> Children read item 1
>
> **a.** (Pass out Storybook.)
> **b.** Open your book to page 165. ✔
> **c.** (Point to the title **rēad the ītem.**) Everybody, touch this title. ✔
> **d.** I'll read the title. You point to the words I read. (Pause.) Get ready. **Read** (pause) **the** (pause) **item.**
> **e.** Your turn to read the title. First word. ✔
> • Get ready. (Tap for each word as the children read *read the item.*)
> **f.** Everybody, say the title. (Pause and signal. Without looking at the words, the children say *read the item.*)
> • (Repeat until firm.)
> **g.** You're going to read the item. Touch item 1 and get ready to read. ✔
> **h.** First word. (Tap for each word as the children read *If the teacher says "Now," hold up your hand.*)
> • (Repeat three times or until firm.)
> **i.** Everybody, get ready to say item 1 with me. (Pause and signal. Without looking at the words, you and the children say:) *If the teacher says* "Now," (pause one second) *hold up your hand.*
> • (Repeat four times or until firm.)
> **j.** All by yourselves. Say item 1. (Signal.) *If the teacher says "Now," hold up your hand.* (Repeat four times or until firm.)
>
> **EXERCISE 24**
>
> Children reread item 1 and answer questions
>
> **a.** Everybody, touch item 1 again. ✔
> **b.** Read item 1 to yourself. Raise your hand when you know what you're going to do and when you're going to do it.
> **c.** (After the children raise their hands, say:) Everybody, what are you going to do if I say **"Now"**? (Signal.) *Hold up my hand.*
>
> > **To Correct**
> > 1. Everybody, read item 1 out loud. (Tap as the children read each word.)
> > 2. What are you going to do if I say **"Now"**? (Signal.) *Hold up my hand.*
>
> **d.** Everybody, when are you going to **hold up your hand?** (Signal.) *If the teacher says "Now."*
>
> > **To Correct**
> > 1. Everybody, read item 1 out loud. (Tap as the children read each word.)
> > 2. When are you going to **hold up your hand?** (Signal.) *If the teacher says "Now."*
>
> **e.** (Repeat *c* and *d* until firm.)

Children play the game

a. Everybody, touch item 1. ✔
b. Read the item to yourself. Raise your hand when you know what you're going to do and when you're going to do it.
c. (After the children raise their hands, say:) Let's play the game. Think about what you're going to do (pause) and when you're going to do it.
d. (Hold out your hand. Pause.) Get ready. **Now.** (Pause. Drop your hand.) *The children hold up their hands immediately.*

---To Correct---
1. What did I say? (Signal.) *Now.*
2. What are you supposed to do if I say **"Now"**? (Signal.) *Hold up my hand.*
3. (If the children's responses are not firm, have them read item 1 aloud.)
4. (Repeat exercise 25.)

Story 152

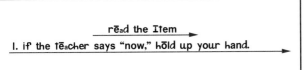

• *Exercise 23, step h.* Pause after the word **now.** This helps the children divide the statement into parts that relate to the two comprehension questions you will ask in exercise 24.
• *Exercise 23, steps i and j.* Be sure the children repeat what they have read at a normal speaking rate.
• *Exercise 24, step b.* Do not insist that the children read silently. They may whisper or read in a low voice.
• *Exercise 24, steps c and d.* Give the children some thinking time in steps *c* and *d*. Hold the last word that you say in step *c*—**nowwww.**

Correction

The corrections for exercises 24 and 25 are specified in the formats. You correct the children by referring them to the item for the answer to the question.

Additional Reading—Independent Readers

Reading Mastery, Grade K: Optional Independent Readers

Both library sets consist of six copies each of five titles. These illustrated books provide children with an opportunity to practice their reading skills as they progress through *Reading Mastery.* The text of each story consists of words that children have learned by the lesson the book is introduced.

The tables below show the lesson to be completed before introducing children to each title.

For *Reading Mastery,* Grade K

Set 1 Titles	Grade K
Sit	70
A Little Fish and His Mom	100
The Goat That Rolled	125
Pat and the Corn	140
The Car	160

For *Reading Mastery,* Grade K

Set 2 Titles	Grade K
In the Sun	70
The Cat Made a Hat	100
Cold	125
Meg and the Nut Loaf	140
The Hill of Hair	160

WORKSHEETS

OVERVIEW

The worksheets support many skills that are taught in the *Reading Mastery* program and shape the children's ability to work independently. Each worksheet presents four or more different activities and will usually occupy the children in independent work for fifteen to thirty minutes. The worksheets also contain the words and stories that the children read from lessons 34 to 90.

The worksheet serves an important function when the children begin to read. It provides parents with a potential basis for praising their child's performance in school. Equally important, it shows parents on a day-to-day basis what is happening in school and what their child is being taught. The worksheet extends and reinforces the teacher-directed activities.

When new worksheet activities are introduced, they are teacher-directed. After two or three days of such direction, the children work on the activities independently. When the children work independently, they should work with as little help from you as possible. Some children may need help with writing early in the program. Work with these children and praise them for progress in working independently.

The Work Check

Check the children's worksheet work each day. Mark errors in pencil or in some way that your marks can be erased so the parent will see a corrected paper. Set up a simple rule that children must have everything corrected on their worksheets before they take them home. Pay close attention to the worksheets. The children's performance on their worksheets reflects how well they have learned a particular skill. If you see a pattern of errors, reteach that skill.

Rewarding the Children

Set up a system of rewards for children who complete their independent work with few errors during the allotted time. Base your rewards on a point system such as the following:

For no errors on the worksheet	10 points
For 1 to 3 errors	2 points
For more than 3 errors	0 points

Make a chart that shows the number of points that each child earns each day. At the end of the week, have an award ceremony at which the children can exchange their points for tangible rewards. These can be inexpensive puzzles or games, class parties at which juice and crackers are served, or special certificates of award that the children can take home, stating that "John earned 26 points this week for hard work on his worksheets."

A reasonable number of points to qualify a child for the awards ceremony is 26.

Summary of Independent Activity

After the children have learned how to do a particular kind of exercise, it becomes part of their independent activity. At the end of each lesson you indicate to the children which worksheet exercises they will complete independently. These activities are specified for you in the last exercises for each lesson.

WORKSHEET TRACK DEVELOPMENT

Each of the worksheet activities shown on the scope and sequence chart on page 86 is developed in a sequence of increasing complexity. The exact steps for teaching these activities are detailed in exercises that appear at the end of each lesson in the Presentation Books.

The exercises from the Presentation Books are self-explanatory, carefully detailed, and easy to follow. You should become familiar with them before teaching the worksheet activities. The first time a new format appears in the Presentation Book, its title has lines above and below it. Follow the directions carefully during the days you present the exercise to the children. Your careful, exact presentation will pay off in fewer errors when the children begin doing the exercises independently.

The following worksheet activities will be discussed in this guide: writing, pair relations, reading comprehension, and story items.

Sound Writing (Lessons 1–160)

The children write sounds every day of the program. They practice the sounds they have already learned.

Worksheet 1

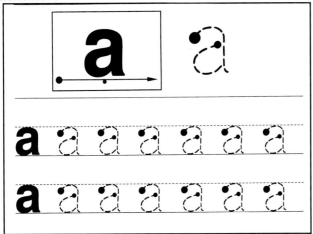

At first you will have to provide additional practice for children who have difficulty forming the symbols. Some of your lower performers may need help in handling a pencil or crayon.

Gradually the sound-writing exercises change so that only a part of the symbol is traced and the rest is done freehand. The change begins at lesson 21.

Worksheet 29

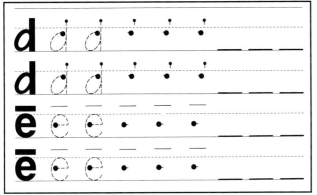

By lesson 40, the children will be making several different symbols freehand on the same sheet.

Story Copying and Sentence Copying (Lessons 40–160)

These worksheet exercises teach the children to copy an entire story, later part of a story, and finally a sentence that is similar to a sentence in the story. In the first exercise, at lesson 40, the children copy directly beneath the story. They trace the letters by following dots on the first line. In early lessons, blocks appear between the words, and there are macrons over the long vowels. All the letters in the words the children write are full-size. Blocks are printed to show the children where they are to write each word.

Worksheet 60

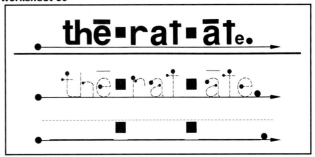

Watch the children carefully to be sure they are writing the letters small enough to fit into the available space. Be sure that they complete one word at a time. The children may try copying a whole row of the first letter, then a row of the next letter, and so on. This defeats the purpose of the exercise—to practice writing whole words.

Starting at lesson 91, children write a sentence related to the story and illustrate it.

The writing exercises reinforce the sounds and words being taught. They are not intended to be a handwriting program.

Pair Relations (Lessons 21–143)

Children who complete the pair-relations exercises are in a good position to understand the kind of workbook activities they will encounter in a variety of school subjects and on standardized tests. For all pair relations, symbols must be paired with the appropriate object or an illustration paired with the appropriate sentence. The examples below show some of the various types of pair-relations exercises in the program.

Worksheet 21

Children complete the pairs.

The purpose of this exercise is to show the children that pairs such as **airplane/m** can be repeated. Each time the pair appears, it must say **airplane/m**.

Worksheet 71

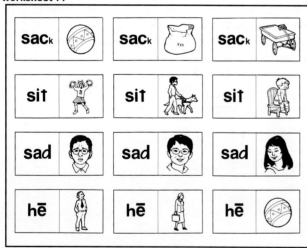

Children cross out the incorrect pairs.

Worksheet 122

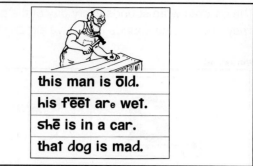

Children draw lines through sentences that do not apply, leaving the correct pair.

Worksheet 126

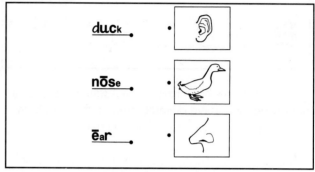

Children complete the pairs.

Reading Comprehension (Lessons 120–160)

The first written reading-comprehension items presented require the children to complete each sentence by circling the appropriate word.

Worksheet 120

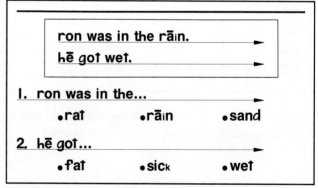

This format extends the skills mastered in the matching exercises, the sentence-saying exercises, and the comprehension exercises presented in connection with reading the story. In picture-completion items, starting at lesson 144, the children use their spelling and comprehension skills to complete two sentences for a given picture.

APPENDIX

SAMPLE LESSONS

Lessons 19 and 108 and their corresponding Storybook and workbook materials are reproduced here in their entirety so that you can practice the skills discussed in this guide before presenting *Reading Mastery* K to your students.

Note: Spelling Lesson 59 is presented the same time as Reading Lesson 108.

PRONUNCIATION
EXERCISE 1

Children say the sounds

a. You're going to say some sounds. When I hold up my finger, say (pause) **ēē.** Get ready. (Hold up one finger.) *ēē.*

b. Next sound. Say (pause) **rrr.** Get ready. (Hold up one finger.) *rrr.*

c. Next sound. Say (pause) **nnn.** Get ready. (Hold up one finger.) *nnn.*

d. (Repeat c for sounds **ēē, rrr,** and **nnn.**)

e. (Call on individual children to do a, b, or c.)

f. Good saying the sounds.

SOUNDS
EXERCISE 2

Sounds firm-up

a. (Point to the column of sounds.) See if you can say all these sounds without making a mistake. (Touch the first ball of the arrow for **a.** Pause one second.) Get ready. (Move quickly to the second ball. Hold.) *aaa.* Yes, **aaa.**

b. (Touch the first ball of the arrow for **s.** Pause one second.) Get ready. (Move quickly to the second ball. Hold.) sss. Yes, **sss.**

c. (Repeat b for each remaining sound in the column.)

d. (Repeat the column until all children are firm on all sounds.)

e. (Call on individual children to say all the sounds in the column.)

f. Good. You said all the sounds in the column.

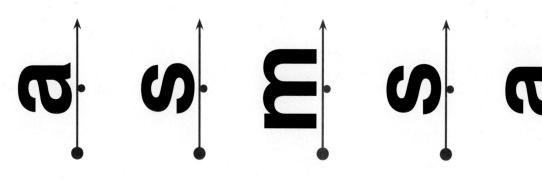

SAY THE SOUNDS—SAY IT FAST
EXERCISE 3

Children say a word or sound slowly, then say it fast

a. I'm going to say some words and some sounds. First you're going to say them slowly. Then you're going to say them fast.

b. Listen. (Hold up a finger for each sound.) Say (pause) **rrraaat.** Get ready. (Hold up a finger for each sound.) *Rrraaat.*

• Again. Get ready. (Hold up a finger for each sound.) *Rrraaat.*

• Say it fast. (Signal.) *Rat.* Yes, **rat.**

c. Listen. (Hold up one finger.) Say (pause) **ĭĭĭ.** Get ready. (Hold up one finger.) *ĭĭĭ.*

• Again. Get ready. (Hold up one finger.) *ĭĭĭ.*

• Say it fast. (Signal.) *ĭ.* Yes, **ĭ.**

d. Listen. (Hold up a finger for each sound.) Say (pause) **zzzooo.** Get ready. (Hold up a finger for each sound.) **Zzzooo.**

• Again. Get ready. (Hold up a finger for each sound.) **Zzzooo.**

• Say it fast. (Signal.) *Zoo.* Yes, **zoo.**

e. (Repeat b through d until firm.)

f. (Call on individual children to do b, c, or d.)

19

Do not show the picture until step *g*, exercise 4.

SAY IT FAST

EXERCISE 4

Children say it fast, then see a picture

a. (Do not show the picture until step *g*.)

b. Say it fast and I'll show you a picture.

c. Listen. **Piiicnic.** (Pause.) Say it fast!
(Signal.) *Picnic.*

• What word? (Signal.) *Picnic.*

d. Yes, what is the picture going to show?
(Signal.) *Picnic.* Yes, **picnic.**

e. In the picture you will see a family in
the park having a . . . (Pause.) **Piiicnic.**
(Pause.) Say it fast! (Signal.) *Picnic.*

f. (Repeat e until firm.)

g. Here's the picture. (Show the picture.)

SOUNDS—SAY IT FAST
EXERCISE 5

Children say a sound slowly, then say it fast

a. (Touch the first ball of the arrow for **s.**) First you're going to say it slowly. Then you're going to say it fast. Say it slowly. Get ready. (Move quickly under each sound. Hold under each sound for one second.) *sssss.*
- (Return to the first ball for **s.**) Say it fast. (Slash.) *s.* Yes, **s.**

b. (Repeat *a* until firm.)

c. (Touch the first ball of the arrow for **a.**) Say it slowly. Get ready. (Move quickly to the second ball. Hold.) *aaa.*
- (Return to the first ball for **a.**) Say it fast. (Slash.) *a.* Yes, **a.**

d. (Repeat *c* until firm.)

e. (Call on individual children to do *a* or *c*.)

SOUNDS
EXERCISE 6

Introducing the new sound ēēē as in ēat

a. (Touch the first ball of the arrow.) Here's a new sound. My turn to say it. Get ready. (Move quickly to the second ball. Hold.) **ēēē.**

b. (Touch the first ball of the arrow.) My turn again. Get ready. (Move quickly to the second ball. Hold.) **ēēē.**

c. (Touch the first ball of the arrow.) My turn again. Get ready. (Move quickly to the second ball. Hold.) **ēēē.**

d. (Touch the first ball of the arrow.) Your turn. Get ready. (Move quickly to the second ball. Hold.) **ēēē.** Yes, **ēēē.**

e. (Touch the first ball of the arrow.) Again. Get ready. (Move quickly to the second ball. Hold.) **ēēē.** Yes, **ēēē.**

f. (Repeat *e* until firm.)

g. (Call on individual children to do *d*.)

h. Good saying **ēēē.**

SOUND OUT

EXERCISE 7

Children say the sounds without stopping

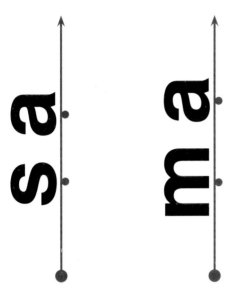

a. (Touch the first ball of the arrow for **sa.**) My turn. I'll show you how to say these sounds without stopping between the sounds. (Move under each sound. Hold. Say **sssaaa.**)

b. (Return to the first ball of the arrow for **sa.**) Your turn. Say the sounds as I touch under them. Don't stop between the sounds. Get ready. (Move under each sound. Hold.) *Sssaaa.*

• (Return to the first ball of the arrow.) Again. Get ready. (Move under each sound. Hold.) *Sssaaa.*

• Good saying **sssaaa.**

c. (Touch the first ball of the arrow for **ma.**) My turn. I'll show you how to say these sounds without stopping between the sounds. (Move under each sound. Hold. Say **mmmaaa.**)

d. (Return to the first ball of the arrow for **ma.**) Your turn. Say the sounds as I touch under them. Don't stop between the sounds. Get ready. (Move under each sound. Hold.) *Mmmaaa.*

• (Return to the first ball of the arrow.) Again. Get ready. (Move under each sound. Hold.) *Mmmaaa.*

• Good saying **mmmaaa.**

e. (Call on individual children to do *b* or *d*.)

SOUNDS
EXERCISE 8

Sounds firm-up

a. (Point to **ē**.) Remember, this new sound is (pause) ēēē.

b. (Point to the column of sounds.) See if you can say these sounds without making a mistake. (Touch the first ball of the arrow for **m**. Pause one second.) Get ready. (Move quickly to the second ball. Hold.) *mmm*. Yes, **mmm**.

c. (Touch the first ball of the arrow for **ē**. Pause one second.) Get ready. (Move quickly to the second ball. Hold.) ēēē. Yes, **ēēē**.

d. (Repeat **c** for each remaining sound in the column.)

e. (Repeat the column until all children are firm on all sounds.)

f. (Call on individual children to say all the sounds in the column.)

g. Good. You said all the sounds in the column.

SAY IT FAST—RHYMING

This is an oral exercise.

Children say word parts slowly, then say them fast

EXERCISE 9

a. Let's do the hard Say It Fast. Listen. (Hold up one finger.) First you'll say (pause) **mmm.** (Hold up second finger.) Then you'll say (pause) **at.**

b. My turn: **mmmat.** Listen again. (Hold up one finger.) First you'll say (pause) **mmm.** (Hold up second finger.) Then you'll say (pause) **at.** Your turn. Say it slowly. Get ready. (Hold up one finger.) *mmm.* (Hold up second finger.) *(mmm)at.*

• Again. Get ready. (Hold up one finger.) *mmm.* (Hold up second finger.) *(mmm)at.* Yes, **mat.**

• Say it fast. (Signal.) *Mat.* Yes, **mat.**

c. (Repeat *b* until firm.)

d. Here's a new word. Listen. (Hold up one finger.) First you'll say (pause) **fff.** (Hold up second finger.) Then you'll say (pause) **un.** (Hold up one finger.) *fff.* (Hold up second finger.) *un.*

e. My turn: **fffun.** Listen again. (Hold up one finger.) First you'll say (pause) **fff.** (Hold up second finger.) Then you'll say **un.** Say it slowly. Get ready. (Hold up one finger.) *fff.* (Hold up second finger.) *(fff)un.*

• Again. Get ready. (Hold up one finger.) *fff.* (Hold up second finger.) *(fff)un.*

• Say it fast. (Signal.) *Fun.* Yes, **fun.**

f. (Repeat *e* until firm.)

g. Here's a new word. Listen. (Hold up one finger.) First you'll say (pause) **zzz.** (Hold up second finger.) Then you'll say (pause) **oo.**

h. My turn: **zzzoo.** Listen again. (Hold up one finger.) First you'll say (pause) **zzz.** (Hold up second finger.) Then you'll say (pause) **oo.** Say it slowly. Get ready. (Hold up one finger.) *zzz.* (Hold up second finger.) *(zzz)oo.*

• Again. Get ready. (Hold up one finger.) *(zzz)oo.* (Hold up second finger.) *(zzz)oo.*

• Say it fast. (Signal.) *Zoo.* Yes, **zoo.**

i. (Repeat *h* until firm.)

j. (Call on individual children to do *b, e,* or *h.*)

WORKSHEET 19

SAY IT FAST
EXERCISE 10

Children say the word fast

a. The word you will say tells what you're going to see on your worksheet. Listen. **Juuummmps.** (Pause.) Say it fast! (Signal.) *Jumps.*

b. Get ready to do it again. Listen. **Juuummmps.** (Pause.) Say it fast! (Signal.) *Jumps.*

c. Yes, the picture on your worksheet will show an animal that really . . . (Signal.) *Jumps.* Yes, **jumps.**

EXERCISE 11

Individual test

a. (Call on each child.) [Child's name], listen. **Juuummmps.** (Pause.) Say it fast! (Signal.) *Jumps.*

b. (Direct each child to the worksheet after child says the word fast.)

SOUND OUT
EXERCISE 12

Children move their finger under **s** or **ē** and say it

a. Everybody, finger on the first ball of the first arrow. ✔
• When I tap, quickly move your finger under the sound and say it. (Pause.) Get ready. (Tap.) *Children move their finger under* **s** *and say* **sss.** Yes, **sss.**

b. Again. Finger on the first ball of the first arrow. ✔
• Get ready. (Tap.) *Children move their finger under* **s** *and say* **sss.** Yes, **sss.**

c. (Repeat *b* until firm.)

d. Everybody, finger on the first ball of the next arrow. ✔
• When I tap, quickly move your finger under the sound and say it. (Pause.) Get ready. (Tap.) *Children move their finger under* **ē** *and say* **ēēē.** Yes, **ēēē.**

e. Again. Finger on the first ball of the first arrow. ✔
• Get ready. (Tap.) *Children move their finger under* **ē** *and say* **ēēē.** Yes, **ēēē.**

f. (Repeat *e* until firm.)

EXERCISE 13

Individual test

a. (Call on a child. Show the child which ball to touch.) Get ready. (Tap.) *Child moves finger under the sound and says it.*

b. (Call on individual children to do *a.*)

c. Good. You really know how to move your finger under the sound and say it.

SOUND OUT

EXERCISE 14

Children touch under the sounds

a. (Hold up side 1 of your worksheet. Touch the first ball of the arrow for **am.**) Put your finger on the first ball of this arrow. ✔ (Put down your worksheet.)

b. What's the first sound you'll say? (Signal.) *aaa.*
• What's the next sound you'll say? (Signal.) *mmm.*

c. Everybody, put your finger on the first ball of the arrow. ✔
• When I tap, you're going to quickly move your finger under each sound and say (pause) **aaammm.** Sound it out. Get ready. (Tap for each sound, pausing about two seconds between taps. Check that children are moving their finger under each sound as they say *aaammm.*)

d. Again. Finger on the first ball of the arrow. Get ready. (Tap for each sound, pausing about two seconds between taps. Check that the children are moving their finger under each sound as they say *aaammm.*)

e. (Repeat *d* until firm.)

EXERCISE 15

Individual test

a. (Call on a child.) Finger on the first ball of the arrow. ✔
• Quickly move your finger under each sound as you say it. Get ready. (Tap for each sound, pausing about two seconds between taps.) *Aaammm.*

b. (Call on individual children to do *a.*)

c. Good moving your finger under each sound and saying each sound.

SOUND WRITING

EXERCISE 16

The children will need pencils.

Children write **ē**

a. (Point to the dotted **ē.**) Everybody, what sound are you going to write? (Signal.) *ēēē.*

b. Get ready to show me the ball you're going to start with. (Pause.) Get ready. (Signal.) *The children touch the big ball.*

c. Put your pencil on the big ball and write **ēēē.** ✔

d. (Point to the top row of dotted **ē's.**) Everybody, now you're going to write **ēēē** in this row until I tell you to stop.

e. (After a minute say:) Stop. You will finish writing **ēēē** later.

SUMMARY OF INDEPENDENT ACTIVITY

EXERCISE 17

Introduction to independent activity

a. (Hold up Worksheet 19.)

b. Everybody, you're going to finish this worksheet on your own. (Tell the children when they will work the remaining items.)
• Let's go over the things you're going to do.

Sound writing

(Point to the sound-writing exercise on side 1.) You're going to finish writing **ēēē.** What are you going to write? (Signal.) *ēēē.*

Cross-out game

a. (Point to the Cross-out Game on side 2.) Here's the Cross-out Game.

b. (Point to the box with the crossed-out **a.**) Everybody, what sound are you going to cross out? (Signal.) *aaa.*

Picture completion

(Point to the picture-completion exercise.) After you do the Cross-out Game, follow the dots and finish this picture. Then you can color it.

END OF LESSON 19

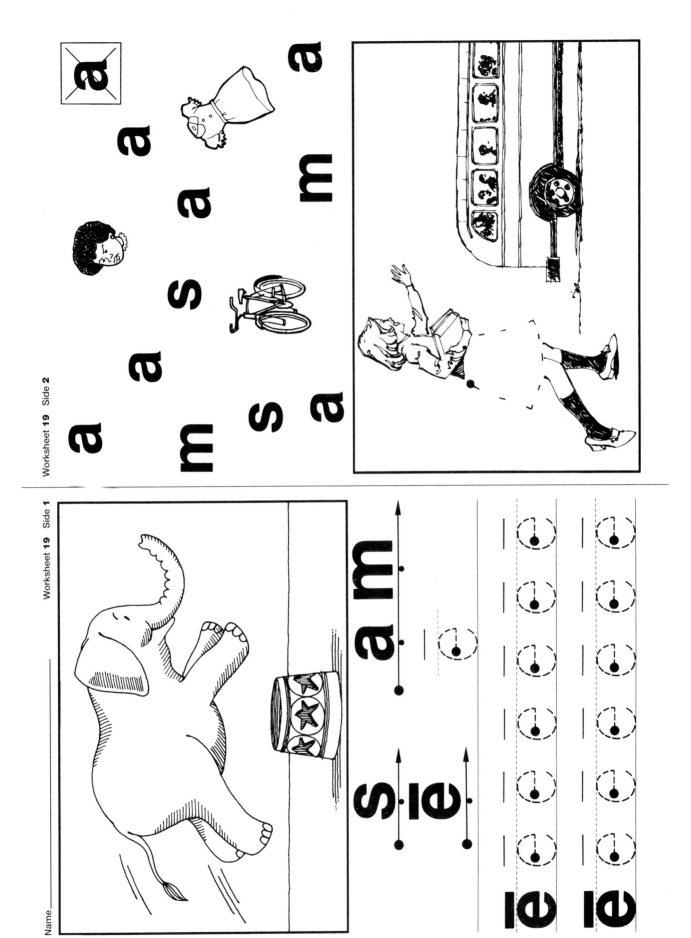

Name

SOUNDS

EXERCISE 1

Teaching **p** as in **pat**

a. (Point to **p.**) Here's a new sound. It's a quick sound.

b. My turn. (Pause. Touch **p** for an instant, saying:) **p.** (Do not say **puuh.**)

c. Again. (Touch **p** and say:) **p.**

d. (Point to **p.**) Your turn. When I touch it, you say it. (Pause.) Get ready. (Touch **p.**) *p.*

e. Again. (Touch **p.**) *p.*

f. (Repeat e until firm.)

EXERCISE 2

Individual test

(Call on individual children to identify **p.**)

EXERCISE 3

Sounds firm-up

a. Get ready to say the sounds when I touch them.

b. (Alternate touching **p** and **d.** Point to the sound. Pause one second. Say:) Get ready. (Touch the sound.) *The children respond.*

c. (When **p** and **d** are firm, alternate touching **p, g, d,** and **t** until all four sounds are firm.)

EXERCISE 4

Individual test

(Call on individual children to identify **p, g, d,** or **t.**)

EXERCISE 5

Sounds firm-up

a. (Point to **p.**) When I touch the sound, you say it.

b. (Pause.) Get ready. (Touch **p.**) *p.*

c. Again. (Repeat b until firm.)

d. Get ready to say all the sounds when I touch them.

e. (Alternate touching **k, v, u, ō, p, sh, h,** and **n** three or four times. Point to the sound. Pause one second. Say:) Get ready. (Touch the sound.) *The children respond.*

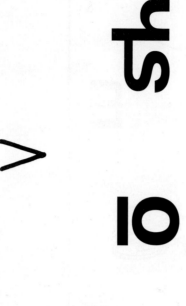

EXERCISE 6

Individual test

(Call on individual children to identify one or more sounds in exercise 5.)

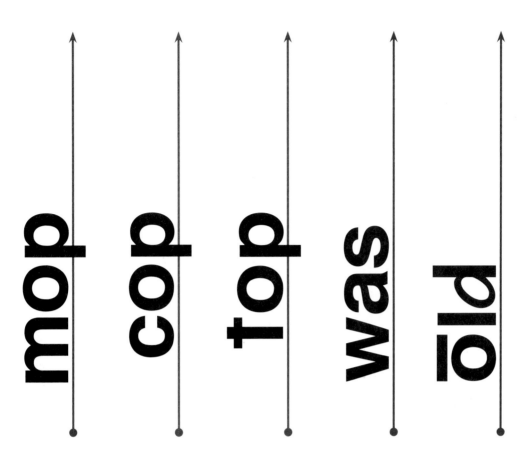

108

READING VOCABULARY

EXERCISE 7

Children rhyme with **mop**

a. (Touch the ball for **mop.**) You're going to read this word the fast way. (Pause three seconds.) Get ready. (Move your finger quickly along the arrow.) *Mop.*

b. (Touch the ball for **cop.**) This word rhymes with (pause) **mop.** (Move to **c,** then quickly along the arrow.) *Cop.*
• Yes, what word? (Signal.) *Cop.*

c. (Touch the ball for **top.**) This word rhymes with (pause) **mop.** (Move to **t,** then quickly along the arrow.) *Top.*
• Yes, what word? (Signal.) *Top.*

EXERCISE 8

Children identify, then sound out an irregular word (**was**)

a. (Touch the ball for **was.**) Everybody, you're going to read this word the fast way. (Pause three seconds.) Get ready. (Move your finger quickly along the arrow.) *Was.* Yes, **was.**

b. Now you're going to sound out the word. Get ready. (Quickly touch **w, a, s** as the children say *wwwaaasss.*)

c. Again. (Repeat *b.*)

d. How do we say the word? (Signal.) *Was.* Yes, **was.**

e. (Repeat *b* and *d* until firm.)

EXERCISE 9

Individual test

(Call on individual children to do *b* and *d* in exercise 8.)

EXERCISE 10

Children read the fast way

(Touch the ball for **ōld.**) Get ready to read this word the fast way. (Pause three seconds.) Get ready. (Signal.) *Old.*

EXERCISE 11

Children read the words the fast way

(Have the children read the words on this page the fast way.)

EXERCISE 12

Individual test

(Call on individual children to read one word the fast way.)

EXERCISE 13

Children identify, then sound out an irregular word (**of**)

a. (Touch the ball for **of.**) Everybody, you're going to read this word the fast way. (Pause three seconds.) Get ready. (Move your finger quickly along the arrow.) *Of.* Yes, **of.**

b. Now you're going to sound out the word. Get ready. (Quickly touch **o, f** as the children say *ooofff.*)

c. Again. (Repeat *b.*)

d. How do we say the word? (Signal.) *Of.* Yes, **of.**

e. (Repeat *b* and *d* until firm.)

f. (Call on individual children to do *b* and *d.*)

EXERCISE 14

Children identify, then sound out an irregular word (**to**)

(Repeat the procedures in exercise 13 for **to.**)

EXERCISE 15

Children read the fast way

(Touch the ball for **that.**) Get ready to read this word the fast way. (Pause three seconds.) Get ready. (Signal.) *That.*

EXERCISE 16

Children sound out the word and tell what word

a. (Touch the ball for **cōat.**) Sound it out.

b. Get ready. (Touch **c, ō, t** as the children say *cōōōt.*)

• (If sounding out is not firm, repeat *b.*)

c. What word? (Signal.) *Coat.* Yes, **coat.**

EXERCISE 17

Children sound out the word and tell what word

a. (Touch the ball for **gōat.**) Sound it out.

b. Get ready. (Touch **g, ō, t** as the children say *gōōōt.*)

• (If sounding out is not firm, repeat *b.*)

c. What word? (Signal.) *Goat.* Yes, **goat.**

EXERCISE 18

Children read the words the fast way

(Have the children read the words on this page the fast way.)

EXERCISE 19

Individual test

(Call on individual children to read one word the fast way.)

of

to

that

cōat

gōat

STORYBOOK

STORY 108

EXERCISE 20

First reading—children read the story the fast way

(Have the children reread any sentences containing words that give them trouble. Keep a list of these words.)

a. (Pass out Storybook.)

b. Open your book to page 37 and get ready to read. ✔

c. We're going to read this story the fast way.

d. Touch the first word. ✔

e. Reading the fast way. First word. (Pause three seconds.) Get ready. (Tap.) *The.*

f. Next word. ✔

• (Pause three seconds.) Get ready. (Tap.) *Old.*

g. (Repeat *f* for the remaining words in the first sentence. Pause at least three seconds between taps. The children are to identify each word without sounding it out.)

h. (Repeat *d* through *g* for the next two sentences. Have the children reread the first three sentences until firm.)

i. (The children are to read the remainder of the story the fast way, stopping at the end of each sentence.)

j. (After the first reading of the story, print on the board the words that the children missed more than one time. Have the children sound out each word one time and tell what word.)

k. (After the group's responses are firm, call on individual children to read the words.)

EXERCISE 21

Individual test

a. I'm going to call on individual children to read a whole sentence the fast way.

b. (Call on individual children to read a sentence. Do not tap for each word.)

EXERCISE 22

Second reading—children read the story the fast way and answer questions

a. You're going to read the story again the fast way and I'll ask questions.

b. First word. ✔

• Get ready. (Tap.) *The̅.*

c. (Tap for each remaining word. Pause at least three seconds between taps. Pause longer before words that gave the children trouble during the first reading.)

d. (Ask the comprehension questions below as the children read.)

After the children read:	You ask:
The old goat had an old coat.	What did she have? (Signal.) *An old coat.*
The old goat said, "I will eat this old coat."	What did she say? (Signal.) *I will eat this old coat.*
So she did.	What did she do? (Signal.) *She ate the old coat.*
"That was fun," she said.	What did she say? (Signal.) *That was fun.*
"I ate the old coat."	What did the goat say? (Signal.) *I ate the old coat.*
"And now I am cold."	What did she say? (Signal.) *And now I am cold.*
Now the old goat is sad.	How does she feel? (Signal.) *Sad.* • Why? (Signal.) *The children respond.*

EXERCISE 23

Picture comprehension

a. What do you think you'll see in the picture? *The children respond.*

b. Turn the page and look at the picture.

c. (Ask these questions:)

1. How does that goat feel? *The children respond.*
   • Cold and sad.
2. Why is she out in the cold without a coat? *The children respond.*
   • Because she ate her coat.
3. Did you ever go outside without a coat when it was cold? *The children respond.*

WORKSHEET 108

SUMMARY OF INDEPENDENT ACTIVITY

EXERCISE 24

Introduction to independent activity

a. (Pass out Worksheet 108 to each child.)

b. Everybody, you're going to do this worksheet on your own. (Tell the children when they will work the items.)

• Let's go over the things you're going to do.

Sentence copying

a. (Hold up side 1 of your worksheet and point to the first line in the sentence-copying exercise.)

b. Everybody, here's the sentence you're going to write on the lines below.

c. Get ready to read the words in this sentence the fast way. First word. ✔

• Get ready. (Tap.) *Thē.*

d. Next word. ✔

• Get ready. (Tap.) *Goat.*

e. (Repeat *d* for the remaining words.)

f. After you finish your worksheet, you get to draw a picture about the sentence, **thē gōat āte thē cōat.**

Sound writing

a. (Point to the sound-writing exercise.) Here are the sounds you're going to write today. I'll touch the sounds. You say them.

b. (Touch each sound.) *The children respond.*

c. (Repeat the series until firm.)

Matching

a. (Point to the column of words in the Matching Game.)

b. Everybody, you're going to follow the lines and write these words.

c. Reading the fast way.

d. (Point to the first word. Pause.) Get ready. (Signal.) *The children respond.*

e. (Repeat *d* for the remaining words.)

f. (Repeat *d* and *e* until firm.)

Cross-out game

(Point to the boxed word in the Cross-out Game.) Everybody, here's the word you're going to cross out today. What word? (Signal.) *Not.* Yes, **not.**

Pair relations

a. (Point to the pair-relations exercise on side 2.) You're going to circle the picture in each box that shows what the words say.

b. (Point to the space at the top of the page.) After you finish, remember to draw a picture that shows **thē gōat āte thē cōat.**

★INDIVIDUAL CHECKOUT: STORYBOOK

EXERCISE 25

2½–minute individual fluency checkout: rate/accuracy—whole story

(Make a permanent chart for recording results of individual checkouts. See Teacher's Guide for sample chart.)

a. As you are doing your worksheet, I'll call on children one at a time to read the **whole story.** If you can read the whole story the fast way in less than two and a half minutes and if you make no more than three errors, I'll put two stars after your name on the chart for lesson 108.

b. If you make too many errors or don't read the story in less than two and a half minutes, you'll have to practice it and do it again. When you do read it in under two and a half minutes with no more than three errors, you'll get one star. Remember, two stars if you can do it the first time, one star if you do it the second or third time you try.

c. (Call on a child. Tell the child:) Read the whole story very carefully the fast way. Go. (Time the child. If the child makes a mistake, quickly tell the child the correct word and permit the child to continue reading. As soon as the child makes more than three errors or exceeds the time limit, tell the child to stop.) You'll have to read the story to yourself and try again later. (Plan to monitor the child's practice.)

d. (Record two stars for each child who reads appropriately. Congratulate those children.)

e. (Give children who do not earn two stars a chance to read the story again before the next lesson is presented. Award one star to each of those children who meet the rate and accuracy criterion.)

41 words/**2.5 min** = 16 wpm [**3 errors**]

END OF LESSON 108

thē ōld gōₐt had an ōld cōₐt.

thē ōld gōₐt said, "I will ēₐt this ōld cōₐt." sō shē did.

"that was fun," shē said. "I ātₑ thē ōld cōₐt. and now I am cōld."

now thē ōld gōₐt is sad.

Worksheet **108**   Side **2**

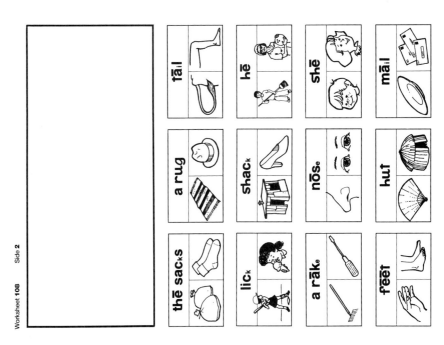

tāil

hē

shē

māil

a rug

shacₖ

nōsₑ

hut

thē sacₖs

licₖ

a rākₑ

fēēt

Name _____

Worksheet **108**   Side **1**

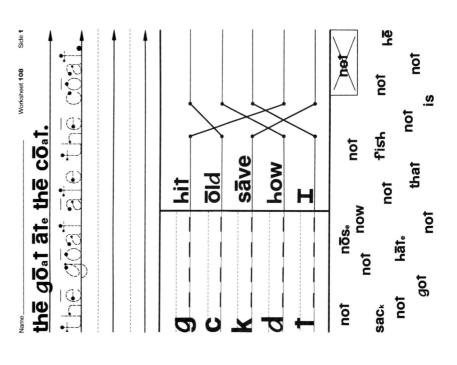

thē gōₐt ātₑ thē cōₐt.

the goat ate the coat

g   hit
c   ōld
k   sāve
d   how
t   I

not   nōsₑ   not
    not   now   fish   not
sacₖ   hātₑ   that   not   hē
    not   got   not   is   not

Reading Mastery Grade K   Teacher's Guide   Sample Lesson 108   77

Spelling Lesson 59

WORD WRITING

EXERCISE 1

Children write **an, ran**

a. You're going to write the word **an**. Think about the sounds in (pause) **an** and write the word. ✔

> **To Correct**
>
> 1. Say the sounds in **an**. (Signal.) *aaannn*.
> 2. Say the sounds the hard way. (Signal.) *aaa* (pause) *nnn*.
> 3. Write the word **an**. ✔

b. (Repeat step *a* for **ran**.)

EXERCISE 2

Children write **dan, tan**

a. You're going to write the word (pause) **dan**. This word is tough. I'll say the sounds in (pause) **dan** the hard way. Listen. **D** (pause) **aaa** (pause) **nnn**.

b. Your turn. Say the sounds in (pause) **dan**. Get ready. (Signal for each sound as the children say:) *d* (pause) *aaa* (pause) *nnn*. (The children are to pause two seconds between sounds.)

• (Repeat until firm.)

c. Everybody, write the word (pause) **dan**. ✔

d. Now you're going to write the word (pause) **tan**. This word is tough. I'll say the sounds in (pause) **tan** the hard way. Listen. **T** (pause) **aaa** (pause) **nnn**.

e. Your turn. Say the sounds in (pause) **tan**. Get ready. (Signal for each sound as the children say:) *t* (pause) *aaa* (pause) *nnn*. (The children are to pause two seconds between sounds.)

• (Repeat until firm.)

f. Everybody, write the word (pause) **tan**. ✔

EXERCISE 3

Children write **sun, fin, nut, mud**

a. You're going to write the word **sun**. Think about the sounds in (pause) **sun** and write the word. ✔

b. (Repeat step *a* for **fin, nut,** and **mud**.)

PRACTICE STORIES

The following pages contain duplicate stories to be used for reteaching children who do not pass Mastery Test 10 (Stories 53, 54, and 55), Mastery Test 12 (Stories 63, 64, and 65), Mastery Test 14 (Stories 73, 74, and 75), and Mastery Test 16 (Stories 83, 84, and 85). The pages may be reproduced for use by your students.

the̅ sad man

mad at me̅

the̅ fat rat

this■ sac k

is■fat.

is■this

a■mitt?

thē■man■is

not■sad.

Worksheet **73** Side **1**

hē ▪ is ▪ an ▪ ant.

hē ▪ has ▪ a ▪ sock

on ▪ his ▪ fēēt.

Worksheet **74** Side **1**

hē ▪ has ▪ an ▪ ant.

that ▪ ant ▪ āte

a ▪ fat ▪ sēēd.

Worksheet **75** Side **1**

hē ▪ āte ▪ a ▪ fig.

and ▪ hē

is ▪ sick.

this · is · a · cat.

this · cat · has · fat

fēēt. · this · cat · can

run · in · thē · mud.

shē · has · a · cat.

that · cat · is

not · littlₑ. · that · cat

is · fat.

hē · has · a · shacₖ.

thē · shacₖ · is · in · thē

sand. · thē · man · is

in · thē · shacₖ.

Student's Name _____ Date_____

Circle 1 point or 2 points if the student answers correctly.

		Part 1				Part 2	
Task 1	step b	0	1 point	Task 1	step a	0	2 points
	step c	0	1 point		step b	0	2 points
Task 2	step b	0	1 point	Task 2	step b	0	1 point
		0	1 point			0	1 point
		0	1 point		step c	0	1 point
		0	1 point			0	1 point
		0	1 point		step d	0	1 point
	step d	0	1 point			0	1 point
		0	1 point				
		0	1 point				
		0	1 point				
		0	1 point				

Part 2 Total Points ☐

Part 1:

Task 3	step b	0	2 points
	step c	0	2 points
Task 4	step b	0	2 points
	step d	0	2 points

Total Points ☐

Number of Points — Part 2

Number of Points	Start At:
0-7	*Reading Mastery,* Grade K, Lesson 11
8-10	If possible, should be placed in *Reading Mastery:* Classic Edition, Fast Cycle.

Number of Points — Part 1

Number of Points	Start At:
0-14	*Reading Mastery,* Grade K, Lesson 1
15-18	*Reading Mastery,* Grade K, Lesson 11 (Circle the lesson)
19-20	Continue testing in part 2, (Check box) ☐

The black number following a word is the lesson in wich the word is introduced in <u>Reading Vocabulary.</u> The blue number is the <u>Story</u> in which it first appears.

a 56
add 41
after 156, 157
al 119
am 48, 40
an 48, 73
and 71, 67
ann 137
ant 69, 73
are 112, 113
arm 115
art 113
as 126
at 43, 43
ate 59, 60
away 158

back 128, 128
bad 146
barn 150, 150
be 126, 134
bean 139
beans 139, 139
bed 126, 128
beds 129
bent 159, 159
better 145, 145
big 126, 126
bike 141
bill 151, 151
bit 126, 126
bite 129, 129
book 152, 154
both 156
box 141, 142
boy 133, 135
boys 139, 140
bring 149
bringing 149
broke 148
broom 144
brother 137, 138
brush 146, 155
brushed 146, 155
brushing 154, 156
bug 123, 126
bugs 126, 127

bus 128, 128
but 127, 129

cake 157
cakes 99, 118
came 73, 113
can 51, 83
cans 139
car 112, 112
card 138, 138
cars 115, 115
cat 50, 83
cats 117, 130
cave 117
caves 116
chicks 123, 123
chip 145
chips 114
chops 113
chore 144
coat 108, 107
coats 107, 107
cold 107, 107
come 140, 148
cop 108, 115
cops 113, 115
corn 119, 119
cow 93, 95
cows 117, 115
cry 160
cut 67

dad 135, 135
dan 48
dark 133, 133
day 146, 146
dear 44
deer 137, 137
did 85, 94
dig 134, 134
digging 134, 134
digs 92
dim 43
dime 144, 144
dip 109
dish 88, 90
dive 130, 131

do 117, 120
dog 110, 112
dogs 121
doing 132
dot 68
down 109, 109
duck 123, 123
ducks 123
dug 134, 134

each 115
eagle 142, 144
eagles 157
ear 32, 124
ears 86, 88
eat 46, 45
eating 125
egg 159
either 147, 147
end 131
even 157, 159
ever 139
every 148

fade 70
fan 50, 51
far 114, 158
farm 114, 115
farms 133
fast 157, 159
faster 160
fat 50, 50
fatter 156, 157
fear 42
feed 34, 119
feel 95, 96
feet 56, 73
fell 159, 152
fig 73, 75
fill 149
filled 152, 152
fin 47
find 135, 137
finding 148
finds 150
fine 151, 135
fish 118, 90
fishing 127, 131
fit 56
five 131
fly 152, 153
fog 110, 113
for 99, 106
fox 141, 142
from 156, 158
fun 66, 77

game 77
games 92
gate 95, 95
gates 95, 95
gave 104, 106
get 120, 120
getting 126, 142
girl 116, 116
girls 130
give 104, 104
go 99, 99
goat 106, 107
goats 107, 115
going 124, 130
gold 152, 152
got 83, 89
gun 136
guns 87

ha 113
had 65, 70
ham 65, 91
hand 76, 142
hands 153
has 68, 72
hat 68, 89
hate 75, 94
hats 89, 103
have 102, 102
having 132
he 63, 67
head 158, 160
hear 111
hears 86
her 138, 137
here 119, 136
hill 91
him 97, 98
his 63, 70
hit 63, 98
hits 97
hitting 142, 142
ho 157
hold 103, 103
hole 134, 134
home 118, 118
hop 140
horse 150, 150
hot 63, 71
how 93, 102
hug 98, 98
hugs 105
hunt 136, 137
hunting 136, 137
hut 70

I 90
if 37, 120
ill 79
in 47, 68
into 133, 133
is 42, 46
it 44, 50
item 151

jump 147
jumped 148, 148
jumps 148

keep 149
kick 97
kicks 97
kiss 98, 98
kissed 124, 124
kitten 101, 101

lake 119, 92
lakes 119
land 76
late 74, 78
leaf 127, 127
leave 147
led 133
leg 145
let 120, 121
let's 127, 127
lick 75, 97
licks 91
lid 79
life 158
lift 122, 122
like 130, 128
liked 151, 141
likes 129
line 134, 151
little 82, 84
live 133
lived 134, 134
lock 76, 79
log 110, 112
logs 126
look 153, 157
looked 156, 156
lot 110
lots 104, 104
love 137, 138
loved 147, 146

mack   62
mad   30, 46
made   70, 90
mail   77, 78
make   158
makes   146
man   52, 53
me   28, 41
mean   49, 139
meat   46, 159
men   122, 122
met   120, 120
mill   79
miss   37
mitt   64, 64
mom   93, 93
moon   145, 148
mop   108
more   119, 127
mother   137, 138
mud   69, 77
must   146, 147
my   152, 153

nail   78
name   59, 81
names   92
near   46, 111
neat   53
need   106, 106
never   139, 146
nine   151, 139
no   98, 98
nod   97
nose   100, 100
not   52, 56
now   91, 91
nut   67, 69
nuts   102

oats   107
of   101, 104
old   100, 103
on   55, 57
or   99, 106
other   137, 143
over   142, 144

paint   122, 124
park   123, 123
part   113
pat   120
pet   121, 121
pets   137
pick   154

picks   158, 160
pie   159, 159
pig   123, 123
pigs   119, 119
pile   145
pond   128, 128
pool   147, 148
pot   112, 112
pots   117, 118

rabbit   131, 132
rack   49
rag   70, 76
rain   75, 77
rake   92
ram   31, 82
ran   48, 51
rat   51, 55
rate   60
rats   98, 149
read   36, 87
red   121, 121
rich   133, 133
ride   136, 136
riding   150, 150
rigs   92
road   114, 114
rock   51, 56
rocks   100, 104
ron   81, 81
ron's   135
room   144, 156
rub   129
rug   70, 72
rugs   105
run   66, 80
runs   86
rut   79

sack   52, 63
sacks   90, 104
sad   30, 47
sag   79
said   89, 94
sail   78
sal   119
sam   37, 59
same   77, 132
sand   75, 85
sat   46, 66
save   102, 104
saves   116
say   160
says   149, 151
seat   57, 111

see   29, 40
seed   33, 74
seem   35
seen   137, 150
sent   121, 138
shack   84, 85
shave   105, 105
she   82, 84
sheep   115
shine   155, 155
ship   109, 118
ships   114
shop   140, 121
shopping   139, 141
shore   143, 143
shot   94
shots   122
show   158
shut   90
sick   56, 67
side   143
sin   68
sit   43, 47
sitting   131, 142
six   153, 155
slam   127
sleep   125, 128
sleeping   127, 142
sleeps   131
slid   132, 132
slide   132, 132
slider   143
sliding   130
slip   127
slipped   154, 156
slow   157, 160
slower   160
smile   155
smiled   155, 156
so   99, 99
sock   55, 73
socks   100, 106
sold   103
some   140, 148
soon   146, 148
sore   132
stand   150, 151
stands   157, 157
start   149, 149
steps   157
stop   129, 134
stopper   141
stopping   133
stops   133
store   147

sun   66, 68
suns   87
swim   148
swimming   148, 148

tack   55
tacks   90
tail   87, 88
take   119, 102
talk   128, 130
talked   145, 146
talking   130, 130
tame   81
tan   49
tar   112, 112
tart   149
teach   115, 116
teacher   149, 151
teaching   154
team   46
tear   45
tears   91
teeth   100, 100
tell   132, 132
ten   127
than   145, 145
that   43, 48
the   42, 44
them   121, 131
then   121, 127
there   120
these   141, 141
they   135, 137
thing   158
things   157, 160
think   160
this   40, 61
those   98
tiger   156, 157
time   132
times   154, 155
tin   47
to   105, 112
told   134, 135
took   154
tooth   154, 155
top   108, 132
topper   141
tops   118, 118
tore   147
touch   153, 155
toy   140, 139
toys   139, 139
tree   156, 157
tub   129, 129

tug   151

under   156, 157
up   122, 122
us   69, 71

walk   128, 130
walked   145, 148
walking   150
was   94, 98
wave   117
waves   116, 133
way   156
we   78, 80
well   126
went   120, 121
wet   120, 120
when   154, 154
where   154
white   154, 155
why   155
wife   158, 159
will   79, 80
win   91
wins   88
wipe   159, 159
wish   89, 90
with   90, 93
wow   94

yard   134, 134
yelled   156, 157
yes   134, 134
you   133, 137
your   150, 152

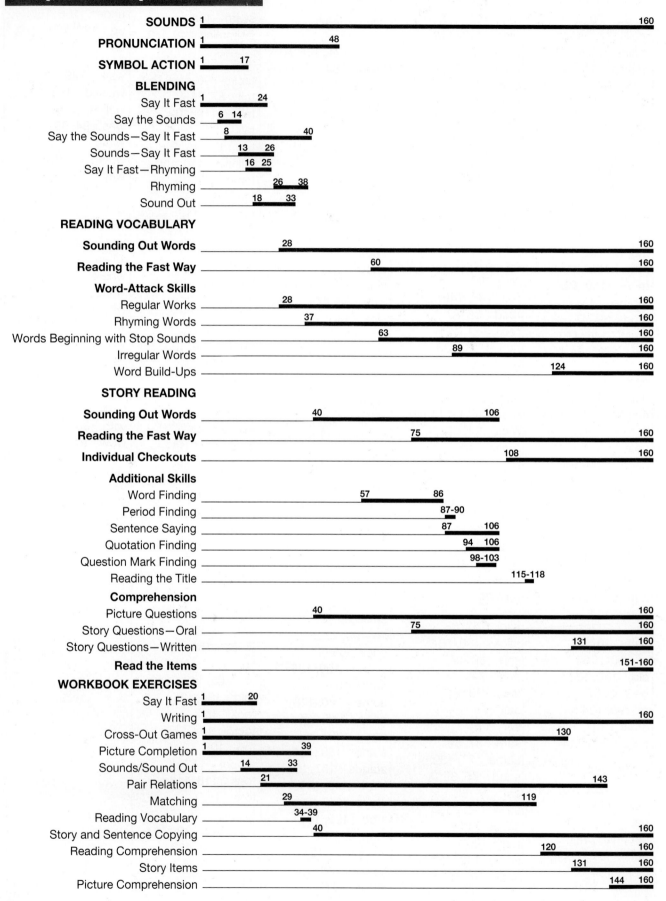

SOUNDS	1 ————————————————————— 160
PRONUNCIATION	1 ————— 48
SYMBOL ACTION	1 — 17
BLENDING	
Say It Fast	1 — 24
Say the Sounds	6 14
Say the Sounds—Say It Fast	8 — 40
Sounds—Say It Fast	13 26
Say It Fast—Rhyming	16 25
Rhyming	26 38
Sound Out	18 33
READING VOCABULARY	
Sounding Out Words	28 ————————— 160
Reading the Fast Way	60 ——————— 160
Word-Attack Skills	
Regular Works	28 ————————— 160
Rhyming Words	37 ———————— 160
Words Beginning with Stop Sounds	63 ——————— 160
Irregular Words	89 —————— 160
Word Build-Ups	124 —— 160
STORY READING	
Sounding Out Words	40 ——————— 106
Reading the Fast Way	75 —————— 160
Individual Checkouts	108 ——— 160
Additional Skills	
Word Finding	57 — 86
Period Finding	87-90
Sentence Saying	87 — 106
Quotation Finding	94 106
Question Mark Finding	98-103
Reading the Title	115-118
Comprehension	
Picture Questions	40 ———————— 160
Story Questions—Oral	75 —————— 160
Story Questions—Written	131 — 160
Read the Items	151-160
WORKBOOK EXERCISES	
Say It Fast	1 — 20
Writing	1 ————————————————— 160
Cross-Out Games	1 ———————————— 130
Picture Completion	1 — 39
Sounds/Sound Out	14 33
Pair Relations	21 ————————————— 143
Matching	29 ————————— 119
Reading Vocabulary	34-39
Story and Sentence Copying	40 ———————————— 160
Reading Comprehension	120 —— 160
Story Items	131 — 160
Picture Comprehension	144 — 160